T0019924

ATLANTIC EDITIONS draw from *The Atlantic*'s rich literary history and robust coverage of the driving cultural and political forces of today. Each book features long-form journalism by *Atlantic* writers devoted to a single topic, focusing on contemporary articles or classic storytelling from the magazine's 165-year archive.

ON
WOMANHOOD

Bodies, Literature, Choice

SOPHIE GILBERT

zando

NEW YORK

ON WOMANHOOD by Sophie Gilbert

Copyright © 2023 by The Atlantic Monthly Group
Introduction copyright © 2023 by Sophie Gilbert

Page 111 is a continuation of this copyright page.

Zando supports the right to free expression and the value of copyright.
The purpose of copyright is to encourage writers and artists to produce
the creative works that enrich our culture. Thank you for buying an
authorized edition of this book and for complying with copyright laws
by not reproducing, scanning, uploading, or distributing this book or
any part of it without permission. If you would like permission to use
material from the book (other than for brief quotations embodied in
reviews), please contact connect@zandoprojects.com.

Zando
zandoprojects.com

First Edition: January 2023

Text and cover design by Oliver Munday

The publisher does not have control over and is not responsible for
author or other third-party websites (or their content).

Library of Congress Control Number: 2022939799

978-1-63893-066-2 (Paperback)
978-1-63893-067-9 (ebook)

10 9 8 7 6 5 4 3 2 1
Manufactured in the United States of America

CONTENTS

INTRODUCTION

When I look at the different pieces assembled in this collection now, what's most striking to me is how many of them were produced after a moment in my life when I knew for certain that I'd never be able to write again. (Sometimes, being wrong is a blessing.) In July 2020—four months into the coronavirus pandemic—I gave birth to twins, an experience that blew up everything, not least of all my brain. During the first two months when I was getting three or four hours of sleep a night, things that used to be instinctual or simple became monumentally hard. Trudging to the coffee shop very early one morning, I was so tired that I momentarily forgot how to walk and had to actively will my legs to lift themselves up, step by step. My fight-or-flight reflexes, primed by evolution to go haywire at even the most minimal threat to the babies, lit up like a pinball machine every time I saw a shadow. It wasn't simple anymore to perceive what was real and what my untrustworthy mind was imagining.

When I went back to work, twelve weeks later, whatever neural pathways I'd once had that allowed me to put words into coherent order were gone. My brain felt distorted and uselessly slow. For months, I'd been fully absorbed in the rigid and oddly mathematical processes of keeping my babies alive; I couldn't read, or watch TV, or do anything that required interpretation or nuance. One night I tried to watch a movie I'd always wanted to see, *Martha Marcy May Marlene*, about a woman who escapes an abusive cult but finds its practices seem to have imprinted on her consciousness and experience of reality. This was, for me, what becoming a mother was like. Who was I before? I couldn't remember. My identity, my desires, my instincts had all been subsumed by the urgency of the present, the heavy mental load of care. A year or so later, I read that the French have an expression for exactly this state of diminishment imposed by motherhood: "femme fondue," or "dissolving woman."

I think it was precisely because my sense of self felt so fractured that when I started trying to write again, my thoughts clustered around how we—people who identify as women—are shaped by external forces before we even begin to know who we are. Before we're born, there are expectations placed on us that offer a powerfully charged direction. Storytelling has always been the primary mode through which those expectations are reified or challenged. And so when I began to think about works of culture again, it was through this particular lens. I used to care most of all about how something made me *feel*— whether it had an emotional resonance that amplified the

A

stakes of trying to exist in this world, the urge to survive and love and be loved. But in this moment, I kept finding myself thinking about frameworks and the invisible architecture supporting the things we think we believe for ourselves. My identity had been so completely upended by circumstance that it made me question how and by what hands it had been defined in the first place.

The pieces in this book coalesce around the notion of womanhood: where it comes from, who controls it, how we are defined by it and define it for ourselves in turn. I haven't written explicitly about trans womanhood in this collection, but trans women are women and the hazards involved in the construction of womanhood apply even more to people who have to constantly affirm their right to exist as woman. The first section considers how women are seen in the world, and how, to quote John Berger, a woman "comes to consider the surveyor and the surveyed within her as the two constituent yet always distinct elements of her identity." The paradigm for ideal womanhood has always been defined by men, whether the medium is novels, music videos, or a *Playboy* centerfold. And the pervasive standards of Western beauty—thin, big-breasted, white—have long left little space for girls to comprehend their value, girls of color least of all. But like so many people, one of the first places I ever truly "saw" myself was within a book. Girls who love stories find freedom to expand their conception of the world and themselves, which is why the historic abuses of men who have power over narrative are so malignant, and so insidious.

The second section in this collection considers how women's stories are told. It's not totally surprising that the marriage plot occupies so much space in fiction: Securing a husband historically was the only path women had toward improving their situation, forging their identity, managing their fate. But its sticky influence in literature is frustrating. The idea that women's noteworthiness as characters ends with marriage seems to double down on the idea that our currency is all about desirability: beauty, sweetness, ownership. The marriage plot, and romantic fiction in general, affirm that love and marriage (and, later, children) are the single most noteworthy things a woman can achieve.

The scope of stories about men is totally different. In literature men do; women often simply *are*. "Girls, enjoined from thinking about becoming generals and emperors, tend to live more in novels than boys do, and to live longer in them," Rachel Brownstein writes in *Becoming a Heroine.* "It is not megalomaniacal to want to be significant; it is only human. And to suspect that one can be significant only in the fantasy of fiction, to look for significance in a concentrated essence of character, in an image of oneself, rather than in action or achievement, is, historically, only feminine." The fantasy of fiction is where we first learn to conceptualize our ambitions. So when I revisited Jackie Collins, one of my teenage self's favorite—and critically derided—authors last year, I was surprised at how radical her books felt now, and how she managed to combine astute, diverse stories about female power and achievement with the emphatic message that women's sexual pleasure matters.

BUT IF SEX HAS always been a battleground, reproduction is its most charged front. In 2018 I wrote about a spate of new works by women authors that were reorienting dystopian fiction around reproductive anxiety and the erasure of women's rights. In the wake of the 2016 election, and with a—reasonable, it turned out—sense of fear around what the reshaping of the Supreme Court might do for women and pregnant people in America, readers were primed for books that crystallized their worst apprehensions. Bina Shah's *Before She Sleeps* imagined a Middle Eastern city in the near future ravaged by a new, fatal strain of HPV, in which surviving fertile women were forcibly married to multiple men. Louise Erdrich's *Future Home of the Living God* told the story of a Native American woman pregnant in a moment when evolution seems to be reversing itself—a forceful metaphor for a country that felt to many women like it was going back-wards in time.

The final section of this book is about that regression, about the power of choice, and the radical potential of actively questioning what we want. Earlier this year I reviewed a book from 1958 about a woman trying to help her 18-year-old daughter procure an illegal abortion, a 65-year-old novel that felt newly relevant in the bleakest way. Similarly, in 2018, I wrote about *Red Clocks*, a novel by Leni Zumas, which imagined, quietly and indelibly, what America without reproductive choice would look like. I wanted to contrast these two pieces with essays about television shows preoccupied with women's bodies, and how being taught to hate our physical selves is a dis-traction from all the other things we could be condemn-ing instead.

Tedious overreliance on rape in a show about dragons, the ubiquity of diet culture—the messaging is pervasive, and hard to shake. But it's all ultimately part of the same impulse as the restrictions on reproductive choice: to deprive women of power, agency, and the ability to sim-ply exist in this world on equal terms. The emotion I've felt more than any other over the last two years has been helplessness. So many of the physical experiences of womanhood, Angela Garbes writes in *Like a Mother*, "reinforce to us that there is little we actually control."

But the ability to shape the narrative in our own terms is a transformative one, as so many of the subjects of these pieces attest.

SOPHIE GILBERT

May 2022

I

SEEN

THE LITERARY-ABUSER
TROPE IS EVERYWHERE

May 2021

IN THE SPRING OF 2021, Eve Crawford Peyton published in *Slate* her account of being groomed and assaulted by the author Blake Bailey. Bailey, she wrote, had been her English teacher in middle school before he held her down and raped her when she was 22, years before he was hand-selected as the most simpatico candidate to tackle a biography of Philip Roth. (Bailey has forcefully denied this and other allegations against him, including that he raped a publishing executive in 2015.) Peyton's account is harrowing, emotive, and masterfully written.

It's also awfully familiar. Bailey, Peyton writes, "was a fantastic teacher; he was a sexual predator." In a 2019 article for *LitHub*, the author Rachel Cline writes about her "groovy, revolutionary, married, draft-evading, girl-raping former teacher," who "taught me how to write," and whom she fictionalized in her novel *The Question Authority*. In her devastating memoir, *Consent*, released in English earlier this year, the French writer Vanessa Springora alleges that a feted French author sexually exploited her as a 14-year-old girl. At one point, she refers to a specific psychological injury: He began to dictate her English homework, replacing her authorial voice with his own in an act she likens to "dispossession." (The author in question, scheduled to stand trial in September for promoting pedophilia, has called the book "unjust and excessive" while praising "the beauty of the love" that he says he and the teenager shared.)

Suddenly, this kind of abuse seems to be everywhere—in the real world and in fiction inspired by it—abuse by men who allegedly found girls who loved books, girls who were conspicuously vulnerable to the written word, and then manipulated and mangled that love in enduring ways. I don't know what to call this new genre, in which women seem to use writing to separate their understanding of abuse from their understanding of language itself. But a genre it is, one whose authors confront a clichéd setup—the predatory teacher or mentor—before they even begin. In Kate Elizabeth Russell's novel, *My Dark Vanessa*, published last year, yet another English teacher grooms a student by giving her books and poems that supposedly remind him of her, offering her "different lenses," she thinks, "to see myself through." In the lead-up to *My Dark Vanessa*'s release, the author Wendy Ortiz noted on Twitter that the book's plot bore striking similarities to her 2014 memoir, *Excavation*, about an English teacher she says exploited her sexually for five years, starting when she was 13 years old. That teacher, like Bailey, and like the man who taught Cline, had his students write journals for class, allowing him to rifle through their innermost thoughts and scrawl in the margins of their imagination. The books aren't similar, but the men depicted in them are.

This is a tricky genre, too, because truth and invention can become so intimately enmeshed. Cline's novel is directly modeled on her experiences with her seventh- and eighth-grade teacher. Russell, after the commotion over *My Dark Vanessa*'s origins led to calls for her to reveal how much of the book was fictional, wrote on her website that it was inspired by her experiences as a teenager, even though she didn't believe that victims should be compelled to share details of traumatic events. Springora's, Ortiz's, and Peyton's accounts are the stark, carefully composed testimony of nonfiction. In Kate Walbert's 2018 novel, *His Favorites*, a charismatic English teacher preys on a student recovering from a tragedy, and his influence on her use of language becomes as insidious as his abuse. Walbert, as far as I can tell, hasn't specified how much of her novel was drawn from real life, but as a teenager she attended the boarding school Choate Rosemary Hall; I can't help but wonder what she made of its begrudging acknowledgment in 2017 that some of its former teachers had abused students for decades.

With narratives like these, the boundaries between truth and fiction are inevitably slippery. "Memory, as you may recall," states Jo, the narrator of *His Favorites*, "is a revision of a revision of a revision, the fortieth draft, or the forty-first." Ortiz echoed this sentiment in an interview with *The Rumpus*: "As soon as I tell a story about a memory, then I'm painting over what actually happened with what I recall." The cloak of a novel can be a kind of self-protection. Meanwhile, biographers, like Bailey, as Ruth Franklin argued in *The New York Times*, "aren't stenographers; we're more akin to novelists, constructing a narrative of a person's life and making editorial choices at every turn." Readers have always relied on writers to interpret the world, to organize it, to humanize its characters, to shape its mordant chaos into something meaningful and enduring. We're only now beginning to see how fragile that trust is, and how easily abused.

AS SHE DESCRIBES IN *Consent*, Vanessa Springora met the writer Gabriel Matzneff (she refers to him throughout only as "GM" or "G") at a dinner party in Paris to which she'd tagged along with her mother, clutching a copy of Balzac's *Eugénie Grandet*. "With my blind veneration of the Writer with a capital W," she writes, "it was almost inevitable that I would conflate the man with his status as an artist." In *His Favorites*, the teacher who torments Jo first notices her while she's clutching a Tolstoy novel in a diner. On the opening page of Lisa Halliday's *Asymmetry*—whose first section many readers have presumed was drawn from the relationship Halliday had in her 20s with Philip Roth—a young woman, Alice, is sitting on a park bench, reading a novel "made up almost exclusively of long paragraphs, and no quotation marks whatsoever," when a very famous, much older writer sits down next to her. "Is that the one with the watermelons?" he asks. Alice hasn't yet come to that part, but a few lines later her cheeks are described as "watermelon pink," as if his influence is already bleeding into her story.

I read *Consent* and *Asymmetry* recently, and I have to note how different they are in scope and style. *Consent* is a blistering indictment of Matzneff—who has written and talked openly about his pedophilia—and of the French literary establishment that tacitly enabled and encouraged his exploitation of children. Springora, who met Matzneff as a 13-year-old who loved to read, has come as an adult to view books with suspicion, she explains in her introduction. "I know they can be poison. I recognize the toxic load they can contain." Matzneff violated her sexually, but he also distorted her relationship with language, art, and education. "At the beginning, G. took me to museums and to the theater, gave me records, told me what books to read," she writes. In his attic apartment, "he would . . . call me his 'beloved child,' his 'beautiful schoolgirl,' and softly recount the long history of illicit love affairs between young girls and middle-aged men. I now had a private tutor entirely dedicated to my education."

Asymmetry is distinct, not least because it's fiction. But it nevertheless expands the idea of what it means to be a young woman in the orbit of a literary legend. Ezra Blazer, the Roth-like elderly author who encounters Alice on the park bench, is written with the lightest of nostalgic touches. He's avuncular and wry. Alice is in her 20s, and fully willing and able to consent to a sexual relationship. Aware of how the pair of them might appear to strangers, she observes that "everything was still more interesting with [Ezra] than without." And yet Ezra woos Alice like a child, with Mister Softee ice-cream cones, boxes of cookies, and Barnes & Noble bags stuffed with books he considers fundamental to her literary education. The novel's title refers to all the power imbalances contained within it—Alice is Ezra's willing companion but not his equal. Although Ezra is not Roth, Halliday explained at a talk in 2018, she wanted to invite readers to think of him, and possibly imagine how a twentysomething woman might have her literary ambitions pruned by what Harold Bloom calls "the anxiety of influence."

To be ensnared by a powerful writer can mean having your sense of self defined by the glare of someone else's commanding gaze. Matzneff, who published diaries and essays as prolifically as novels, wrote about Springora and cast her as yet another character in his work. He encouraged her to write him love letters, which she eventually realized sounded similar to all the other letters from girls he published in his work. "These weren't words of contemporary young women, but the universal and timeless terms taken from the epistolary literature of love," Springora writes. "G. whispered them to us by stealth, breathing them onto our very tongues. He dispossessed us of our own words." All the while, he was also crafting a defense against allegations that might stain him in the future. "All these declarations of love were proof that he was loved, and better still, that he knew how to love," Springora continues. "What a hypocritical way it was of going about things, deceiving not only his young mistresses but also his readers."

Alice, on the other hand, isn't trapped within Ezra's fiction in *Asymmetry*, but he does impose constraints on her work before she's even confessed a desire to make it. "I know what you're up to," he tells her one day in the park. "I know what you do when you're alone . . . You're writing. Aren't you?" He assumes immediately that she's writing about their relationship, because who wouldn't? Why write if not to develop and enshrine one's own ideas, experiences, and impressions? But Alice's interests lie outside the scope of her own psyche. "Writing about myself doesn't seem important enough," she tells him. Ezra's gaze is turned inward; whether you, the reader, assume that he is Roth-inspired or merely Roth-like, you know he's never found himself lacking in importance. The second section of *Asymmetry*, which abandons Ezra and Alice entirely to feature the first-person narrative of an Iraqi American economist detained at Heathrow Airport, by contrast, feels like nothing so much as a scrupulous rejection of Ezra's advice; when readers learn that it's written by Alice years later, it comes off as an act of authorial empathy and imagination. Alice's relationship with Ezra may have been pleasurable and consensual, yet her writing, and Halliday's, is an act of literary sedition.

Consent, too, is an expression of rebellion, and power. Springora had dreamed of revenge against Matzneff, she writes, and one day "the solution finally presented itself to me, like something that was completely obvious: Why not ensnare the hunter in his own trap, ambush him within the pages of a book?" Methodically, with brutal emphasis, she also savages the people complicit in her abuse: her mother, who eventually seems to have sanctioned her 14-year-old daughter's "relationship" with a famous writer because of his cachet; the publishers and editors, who fostered and funded a self-confessed predator; the police, who she says investigated at the time and did nothing; the doctor, who offered to surgically sever her hymen so that Matzneff could penetrate her; the teacher, who cornered her in a bistro one day and told her of his admiration for Matzneff while ogling her breasts; the famous writer, who told her that her role was to bow to Matzneff's impulses and help him create. "Literature is all about lying, my dear young friend," the writer tells her. "Didn't you realize?"

THE MANIPULATION OF LANGUAGE is the common thread sewn through each of these books. Springora includes a quote by the novelist Chloé Delaume at the beginning of her memoir's final section: "Language has always been an exclusive domain. Who owns language owns power." In one scene in *His Favorites*, Jo reports her teacher to the headmaster, who dismisses her. She thinks in hindsight that she should have responded by blasting his patriarchal fossilization into powder, but remembers that she was only 15 at the time. "I could no more have formed those words, those thoughts, than flown to the moon." Springora describes in one chapter feeling as if she's no match for Matzneff because she doesn't yet have the words she needs to challenge him:

> I wasn't familiar with the terms "narcissistic per-vert" and "sexual predator." I didn't know there was such a thing as a person for whom the Other does not exist. I still believed that violence was only ever physical. And G. manipulated language like others manipulate swords . . . It was impossi-ble to do battle with him on equal terms.

Similarly, in *My Dark Vanessa*, the influence of the teacher who abused Vanessa is so profound even in adulthood that it's obvious to the reader when she's parroting his words in her narrative instead of forming her own assessments. "There was something about me that made it worth the risk," she thinks. "I had an allure that drew him in." She rejects the word *abuse* to describe what happened to her, because "in someone else's mouth the word turns ugly and absolute. It swallows up everything that happened." The simple integrity of a word cuts through the fog of her self-delusion. But she also twists language to deceive herself. To be groomed, she thinks, suddenly pedantic about definitions, "is to be loved and handled like a precious, delicate thing."

Peyton's account of how Bailey allegedly groomed his students includes the information that he required his students to keep personal journals and submit them to him; he would respond in red ink, positioning himself as a kind of omniscient narrator, armed with all the intimate details of his students' psyches. In one girl's yearbook, according to a reported *Slate* story that accompanied Peyton's essay, Bailey wrote, "Mr. Antolini to Holden; me to you," a reference to *The Catcher in the Rye* that implied she had disappointed him by distancing herself from him. (In *The Question Authority*, Nora, the central character, recalls how she once tried to write like J. D. Salinger in the journals she turned in for class; her teacher, Mr. Rasmussen, scribbled, "Nice try, Phoebe," in the margins.) Bailey also reportedly told the same student to "unfasten your gaze from your own navel," perhaps a caustic way of suggesting that she herself bore no value as a subject or as a person.

What I take from *Consent* and its cohort of books—and from the ways they play with language, with perspective, with myopia and clarity—is how neatly they balance exposing abusers with a radical reframing of subject and object. The *New Yorker* editor David Remnick wrote in March about the "predatory dimension of one person telling the story of another." But when you're telling a story *about* a predator, this dynamic gets fundamentally subverted. When Roth, in the last interview he gave before his death, was asked about the #MeToo movement, his response was to explain how consistently over the course of his career he'd written about "men enveloped by sexual temptation." He had, he said, "stepped not just inside the male head but into the reality of those urges whose obstinate pressure by its persistence can menace one's rationality, urges sometimes so intense they may even be experienced as a form of lunacy." I don't know whether Roth was a misogynist. (It is fascinating that he supposedly chose Bailey after a shared backslapping moment over the sexual appeal of Ali MacGraw.)

But it is easy to say who attracted Roth's interest, and who didn't. Men in compulsive sexual thrall: interesting. Women violated as a result: far less so. And yet here are women, writing books, forcing their perspectives into the light, and proving what potent, insurgent art can be made in the process.

THE PROBLEM WITH EMILY RATAJKOWSKI'S *MY BODY*

November 2021

REWATCHING THE MUSIC VIDEO FOR "Blurred Lines," the totemic Robin Thicke song, is an interesting project. In 2013, when it was released, the song spawned a new microeconomy of commentary denouncing it as a distillation of rape culture, or fretting over whether enjoying its jaunty hook was defensible. ("I know you want it," Thicke croons presumptively over and over, even though honestly, no, I do not want it at all.) In the video, directed by the veteran Diane Martel, three models dressed in transparent thongs peacock and pose with a baffling array of props (a lamb, a banjo, a bicycle, a four-foot-long replica of a syringe) while Thicke, the producer and one of the co-writers Pharrell Williams, and the rapper T.I. dance, goofy and fully clothed, around them.

As an artifact of its time, it's a remarkably deadened and nonsensical thing. But what most surprises me now is how pitiable the men seem, pulling at the models' hair and playing air guitar for attention, less musical superstars than jejune dads who don't exactly know what to do with the women they've paid to be naked. This is the raw power of the female body, and yet what kind of power is it, really? At one point, Thicke seems to push the model Emily Ratajkowski against a wall, hollering into her ear while she gazes away from him, a picture of barely suppressed disdain.

"Blurred Lines" instantly made Ratajkowski a star. She commands the video in both the PG-13 and unrated versions like a supernova, a vortex of pulchritude and screen presence and sticky red lip gloss. "They were the talent; we were more like props," Ratajkowski writes of the men in her new book, *My Body*, and yet the women are the ones viewers can't look away from. They're so casual in their nudity, so composed, so unperturbed by the antics of the men objectifying them. Their sexuality seems to exist somehow outside the range of the camera's gaze, outside the atmosphere of mortal men. But, of course, it doesn't. In *My Body*, a collection of essays in which Ratajkowski scrutinizes the blessing and the curse of her physical self, she writes that Thicke groped her during filming that day, and that she said nothing; the incident was, in her eyes, a reminder of "how limited any woman's power is when she survives and even succeeds in the world as a thing to be looked at." (Thicke has not publicly responded to the allegations.)

This book is Ratajkowski's attempt to come to terms with her existence as a person who is, in the words of

A

Derek Zoolander, really, really ridiculously good-looking. This experience is, she knows, particularly fraught for women and girls. Starting in middle school, Ratajkowski writes, she received mixed messages about her body—whether it provoked offense or pleasure, was too big or too small, made her strong or vulnerable. Commodifying it as a model at first brought her satisfaction. She writes: "All women are objectified and sexualized to some degree, I figured, so I might as well do it on my own terms. I thought that there was power in my ability to choose to do so." Now? She's not so sure, but nor has she entirely changed her mind.

My Body sits in this liminal space between reappraisal and self-defense. It's a fascinating work: insightful, maddening, frank, strikingly solipsistic. Ratajkowski admits in her introduction that her awakening is still a half-finished one, and that the purpose of the book wasn't "to arrive at answers" about the contradictions of selling her own image as a model, actor, and Instagram influencer with 28.5 million followers, but rather to "examine the various mirrors in which I've seen myself." She senses, maybe, that she's caught in an age-old quagmire (what the academic Sandra Bartky called "the disciplinary project of femininity"), but not that she's become, by virtue of her fame and self-presentation, potentially complicit in the things she critiques. Writing, for Ratajkowski, seems to let her assert the fullness of her personhood and interiority, a rejection of the world's determination to make her an object. But the narrowness of her focus—her physical self, essentially, and everything it's meant for her—is limiting. Even her title, *My Body*, suggests conflicting things: ownership and depersonalization. What do you do when the subject you know best, the topic upon which you are the ultimate authority, is the same trap you're trying to write your way out of?

THE DAY I READ most of this book was also the day that Ratajkowski uploaded to Instagram a series of photos published by the French magazine *M*. In the first, she holds a flesh-colored lollipop against her tongue. The third reveals her midriff, her nipple, and her leopard-patterned nails, but not her face. The cover line for the shoot reads: *La Feminité à l'Offensive*, with *faux cils et ongles longs* in smaller type, just to clarify that the aesthetic for the revolution is false eyelashes and long fingernails. Ratajkowski's waist is tiny; her ribs are visible; her lips are pursed.

She has the right to find these pictures, this self-presentation, empowering. ("I love these images so much!" her caption reads.) But we also, as observers, have the right to interpret them—to wonder if doubling down on archaic tropes of female sexuality and the "tyranny of slenderness," as Bartky put it, is actually good for anyone

A

else. In her book's epigraph, Ratajkowski pulls a quote on vanity from John Berger's *Ways of Seeing*, a seminal BBC series and book that, among other things, crystallizes the bind women find themselves in as objects to be surveyed. The *M* pictorial made me think of a different Berger argument: Portraits are organized to reinforce the hierarchical status quo, and the women within them are arranged, he wrote, "to feed an appetite, not to have any of their own." Whose appetite is the lollipop feeding? What message about empowerment can it possibly convey? Does it matter?

Ratajkowski doesn't say much in the book about how women and girls might respond to images of her. That myopia is frustrating, because she's so astute on the subject of how her body is interpreted by men. The project that became *My Body* began as an essay published last year in *New York*. In "Buying Myself Back," the magazine's most read story of 2020 (not exactly a quiet news year), Ratajkowski wrote about being sued by a paparazzo who took a picture of her on the street after she subsequently posted the photo on her Instagram, and buying half a Richard Prince "Instagram painting" based on an image of herself. She also alleged that she was sexually assaulted by a photographer who later published a book of nude photos of her without her consent. (The photographer denied the accusations to *New York*, saying, "You do know who we are talking about right? This is the girl that was naked in *Treats!* magazine, and bounced around naked in the Robin Thicke video at that time. You really want someone to believe she was a victim?")

The essay was bracing and sharp. It distilled in careful prose the absurdity and powerlessness of being a product in the internet age. "I have learned that my image, my reflection, is not my own," Ratajkowski writes. To cope, she starts to think of herself in split form: the "real" Emily and the one whose picture is appropriated by men in ways she can't control. If Marx were alive, he might refer her to his theory of alienation: Under capitalism, Ratajkowski has essentially lost control of the work she produces, and her sense of self is fragmenting as a result. (Even Marx might be stunned by the audacity of Prince charging $80,000 for a picture he ripped right off Instagram and modified merely with the addition of his own sleazy comment.)

That Ratajkowski's response to so much injustice might be to seize back control (and the means of production) for herself is understandable. But burning down a house that you are still very much inside is hard, which is maybe why so much of the rest of *My Body* feels impotent. It's less a rallying cry for structural change than a dispassionate series of observations by someone who still sees themselves primarily as a commodity. Its tone is measured

A

and numb. In the essay "Bc Hello Halle Berry," the author develops headaches during a stay in a luxury Maldives resort paid for by a Qatari billionaire (in return for some Instagram uploads). As she posts a photo of herself wearing a bikini from her own line, only slightly mollified by the hundreds of thousands of likes it receives in under an hour, she ponders the ethics of using her body for profit. "Money means power," she thinks. "And by capitalizing on my sexuality I have money. The whole damn system is corrupt and anyone who participates is just as guilty as I am . . . I have to make a living somehow."

It seems uncharitable to point out that she's drawing a false dichotomy—that there are options in between trading pictures of herself for free vacations and starving on the street. But that's not the point. The issue that kept sticking with me as I read was that Ratajkowski so clearly wants to have it all: ultimate control over the sale of her image; power; money, yes; but also kudos for being more than an object, for being able to lucidly communicate how much she's suffered because of a toxic system—and is still suffering because of her ongoing participation. It is, as they say, a lot to ask.

To her credit, Ratajkowski seems to occasionally sense the innate hypocrisy of her desires, her impulse "to have my Instagram hustle, selling bikinis and whatever else, while also being respected for my ideas and politics and well, everything besides my body." In the essay "Beauty Lessons," a recollection of how her priorities and self-esteem were shaped in part by a mother with her own internalized misogyny, Ratajkowski recalls learning as a child that the suffering attractive women endure at the hands of the world "was actually a good thing, a consequence of being beautiful and having access to male attention." The world, she realizes, "isn't kind to women who are overlooked by men." When she starts modeling, she can't remember ever actually enjoying the process of it, but she does enjoy the money she's able to make, and the things she can buy. But the industry and its nebulous edges also present new compromises. In the essay "Transactions," Ratajkowski writes about being paid $25,000 in 2014 to go to the Super Bowl with a Malaysian financier, a deal brokered by her manager at the time. She's troubled by the "unspoken task I'd been hired to perform: to entertain the men who had paid me to be there." To be a beautiful woman, she seems to conclude, is to exist in the hustle between obligation and power, this particular "spectrum of compromise."

Becoming an author allows her to reject this setup. Writing a book that's effectively a literary portrait of your own physical self, though, is to risk reinforcing all the preconceptions anyone has ever had about you. Ratajkowski is a graceful and thoughtful writer, and as I read her book I longed for her to turn her gaze outward, to write an essay about marriage plots or coffee or landscape architecture or *Scooby-Doo*. Or, beyond that, I wanted her to risk fully indicting modeling as a paradigm—to not merely note that her career took off after she lost 10 pounds from stomach flu and kept the weight off, but to probe what looking at images of so many skinny bodies all day does to girls as delicate and unformed as her own teenage self. To think more explicitly about the fact that, as Tressie McMillan Cottom elucidates in her essay collection, *Thick*, "beauty isn't actually what you look like; beauty is the preferences that reproduce the existing social order." To wonder not just how the inherently flawed bargain of modeling has damaged her, but how it damages everyone. To risk letting herself feel or uncover something that might be a catalyst for not just observation, but transformation.

What would that kind of growth cost her? At the very least, perfection. In her final essay, "Releases," Ratajkowski writes about how she has long resisted anger because she sensed that anger makes women physically repulsive. "I try to make anything resembling anger seem spunky and charming and sexy," she writes. "I fold it into something small, tuck it away. I invoke my most reliable trick—I project sadness—something vulnerable and tender, something welcoming, a thing to be tended to."

Thinking about women's emotions being modulated by the primacy of staying sexy isn't exactly new, but it's dismaying all the same. If Ratajkowski still can't get angry, unpleasantly angry, even in writing, for fear of sacrificing her power, what about the rest of us?

CURSE OF THE '90S BOMBSHELL

February 2022

THE HULU MINISERIES *Pam & Tommy* could have had a fascinating focus. We see glimpses of it in the first minute, on a grainy TV screen where Jay Leno (played by the comedian Adam Ray) is interviewing Pamela Anderson (Lily James). "Speaking of sex, and I have to ask," Leno says, throwing his hands up and down in the faux-innocent shrug of someone *just asking questions*. "The tape." The audience audibly inhales. Anderson, whom James imitates in uncanny fashion—the protruding tongue, the hands perched nervously on crossed legs, the slightly hunched posture—plays similarly dumb. "What tape, Jay?" she breathes. Leno casually twists the knife. "What's that like?" he says. "What's it like to have that kind of exposure?" The camera zooms in on Anderson's pained face as she grapples with her response.

The choice to mediate our first glimpse of Anderson through multiple screens is, perhaps, telling; it has a distancing effect that keeps her at arm's length. *Pam & Tommy* is an eight-part miniseries about how an intimate home movie—made by Anderson and her then-husband, the rock star Tommy Lee, on their honeymoon—became the first viral celebrity sex tape. With the Leno scene, the show suggests sensitivity for Anderson's plight (the tape was stolen by an irate contractor and sold online without her consent). Then it abruptly changes course. The scene that follows, set one year earlier, shows a carpenter, Rand Gauthier (Seth Rogen), trying to focus on construction work in a Malibu mansion as Anderson and Lee (Sebastian Stan) go at it loudly upstairs. This is how the series really sees Anderson: Woman Victimized by the Culture, but also Woman Unabashedly Banging Her Heart Out.

Pam & Tommy, notably, hasn't been sanctioned by Anderson, who has ignored all attempts by the series' writers and stars to get in touch with her, and who is reportedly distressed by yet another distillation of her life and career down to the moment when she was most appallingly exploited. In response, the show's lead director, Craig Gillespie (*I, Tonya*), has said that reclaiming Anderson's narrative was part of the point of the series—that the people involved "absolutely respect [her] privacy" and wanted to use the series to change the "perspective of what happened."

Really? I don't necessarily doubt the good intentions of the showrunners, Robert Siegel and D. V. DeVincentis, and their show—in moments—does succeed at communicating the ordeal Anderson endured and the many different forces that colluded in her suffering. But you're not respecting her privacy when you re-create a sex tape that was stolen and viewed by hundreds of millions of people without her permission. You aren't reclaiming her narrative on her behalf if she insists that she doesn't want you to do so. The show's creators would be better off just stating the truth: They wanted to tell Anderson's story because it's a good story, and its revelations have deeply informed the mess of celebrity and internet culture that we wallow in today. Even the fact that she resisted participating in the show is telling: What Anderson wants for herself has always mattered less than the desires she incites in others.

CRITIQUING *Pam & Tommy* as a single, unified work is hard because it's such an awkward hybrid of genres and ideas. Based on a 2014 *Rolling Stone* story about Gauthier, the contractor with a grudge who accidentally introduced revenge porn to mainstream America, it's equal parts caper, raunch comedy, romance ("the greatest love story ever sold" is the tagline), and cultural analysis. A scene in which Lee converses with his puppetized penis (voiced by Jason Mantzoukas) is ripped right from his memoir but feels derivative of *Big Mouth*. Meanwhile, an episode about a legal deposition Anderson gives while suing *Penthouse*—written by Sarah Gubbins (*Shirley*, *Better Things*) and directed by Hannah Fidell (*A Teacher*)—straightforwardly parses all the ways

Anderson was ritualistically humiliated in the '90s for daring people to look at her.

The first episode hardly features Anderson at all. It's focused on the conflict between Gauthier—like so many Rogenite heroes, an endearing naïf whose interests include marijuana and masturbation—and Lee, who's hired him to manifest a project the rock star has envisioned as a "fucking futuristic, state-of-the-art love pad 2000." Lee is an unexploded bomb. The puppeteer Frank Oz once said that Animal, the frenzied drummer he performed as on *The Muppet Show*, could be summed up in five words—*drums, sleep, sex, food,* and *pain*—and the same goes for Stan's portrayal of Lee, with trunkfuls of pharmaceuticals thrown into the mix. The Mötley Crüe drummer is heavily tattooed, priapic, and . . . surprisingly sweet? To watch *Pam & Tommy* after living through the tabloid coverage of their relationship—the beach wedding, the hepatitis, the kids, the breakup, the domestic abuse, the jail sentence, the reunions—is to feel uncomfortably like you're rooting for them, these crazy kids who take endless baths, are dying to have a family together, and don't have sex until their wedding night (four days after their first date).

Their downfall, though, is inevitable. After Lee fires Gauthier and waves a shotgun in his face, Gauthier, an "amateur theologian," decides that karma is taking too long and cooks up a revenge plot. He cases the Malibu home for several weeks, breaks in one night, and steals a safe, which contains cash and jewelry, numerous guns, and an unmarked video tape. That tape, he discovers, contains an explicit home movie filmed on a yacht during Anderson and Lee's honeymoon. He shows the tape to a porn director he knows, Milton "Uncle Miltie" Ingley (Nick Offerman, in fine sober-unhinged form), who immediately appraises its value. "This is so private," Ingley says. "It's like we're seeing something we're not supposed to be seeing . . . which is kind of what makes it so fucking hot."

The pair's efforts to monetize the tape allow the show to make broader points: The series positions the Anderson-Lee video as not just a debauched tabloid frenzy, but a moment that actually changed the world—a fracturing of established mores in American life (about privacy, sex, celebrity, commerce) at the hands of the internet. Here was a new, unregulated marketplace without any standards or legal precedents. The porn industry at the time required signed releases to sell videos of adults engaging in sexual intercourse; the internet meant that Gauthier could sell the tape he'd stolen without restriction. But it meant that anyone else could too. What had been a business was now suddenly a free-for-all for anyone with an explicit video and an agenda. (Siegel, *Pam & Tommy*'s co-showrunner, seems intrigued by historical turning points in American capitalism—he wrote the script for *The Founder*, the story of how Ray Kroc ruthlessly turned McDonald's into an incomparable business empire.)

Naturally, this shift was bad news for women. The way *Pam & Tommy* tells the story doesn't so much reclaim her narrative as manipulate it to draw bigger conclusions about what the internet age, the proliferation of cameras everywhere, and the erosion of privacy would mean not just for celebrities, but for all women. The major beats of her life story are there: her "discovery" at a football game, her first audition for *Playboy*, her elevation to icon status via a prime-time beach soap and a strategically tailored red bathing suit. James looks so similar to Anderson in some scenes that the lines between truth and fiction seem to wobble a little. And the English actress captures what may be the heart of Anderson: She describes herself, in one early scene, as just "a good Christian girl from small-town Canada," and she's resolutely sweet and courteous to almost every person she meets. But in *Pam & Tommy*, Anderson comes to represent more than herself— she's an avatar for every woman who's ever been slut-shamed or abused, or who's ever suffered a loss too poignant to bear. She's a foil for men like Gauthier to have their own moments of revelation. "Oh man, I feel terrible for women," he tells his ex-wife (Taylor Schilling), a character patently created for these kinds of discussions. "They gotta deal with us."

For Anderson, maybe the fact that she's less a person in the show than a collection of tropes and stories—the misunderstood bombshell, the innocent in love, the icon

A

wronged by the media—animated into a whole is some consolation. But I doubt it. The more we rely on these narratives of '90s revisionism to confront the flaws in our own past thinking, the more responsibility we have to wonder who's being served in the process. Is it right to take a painful invasion of privacy that was turned into mass entertainment and turn it into mass entertainment again, even if the motivations have changed? Have they changed? I enjoyed this show. It made me think about Anderson differently—as someone who's survived extraordinary victimization and typecasting *and* who's managed to redefine how she's perceived. (Whether steadfast defender of Julian Assange trumps *Baywatch* babe depends on your worldview, I guess.) But the series, which so often feels like it's trying to atone for our old mistakes, seems intent on pointing out ethical transgressions while looking right past the notable void at its own core.

THE UNENDING
ASSAULTS ON GIRLHOOD

———————

March 2021

GIRLHOOD, MELISSA FEBOS WRITES IN her new essay collection of the same name, is "a darker time for many than we are often willing to acknowledge." The overall impression she creates is a collage of discomfitingly familiar rites of passage, all distinct and yet all tied together by a thread of learned self-abnegation. The book reads at moments like a meme built from various half-buried abuses and indignities, in which you pick the ones that apply to you—"Tag yourself. I'm *Sexually Harassed as a Teenager by My Middle-Aged Boss*, but also *Stalked on the Way Home From School* and *Consented to Acts I Didn't Want to Do to Avoid a Worse Outcome*." Febos is an intoxicating writer, but I found myself most grateful for the vivid clarity of her thinking. During girlhood, she argues, "we learn to adopt a story about ourselves—what our value is, what beauty is, what is harmful, what is normal—and to privilege the feelings, comfort, perceptions, and power of others over our own."

The week I read this book, in March 2021, seven women and one man were murdered in Atlanta by a man who seems to have resented his desire for women so much that he decided to kill some of them, privileging his comfort over their lives. That same week, a document drawing from hundreds of reports alleging rape, assault, and harassment at my London high school and its brother institution was made public. The file, an open letter to the headmaster of the boys' school, Dulwich College, is filled with stories of violations both large and small that girls minimized because, like Febos, they were taught extremely early on to protect boys from the reality and the consequences of their behavior. The document is painfully long; each story tore at my heart and made me burn with useless rage.

I haven't vetted the stories and don't know whether they're all true. (The school's headmaster responded by condemning the attitudes and behavior detailed in the letter, and he has since passed on allegations against specific students to the police.) But they track with my experiences, and with those of the women I've spoken with who attended my school over the past three decades. Woven throughout the accounts is an ingrained acceptance among all parties that this is just the way things are, and that questioning it is pointless. "I pretended I was asleep," one young woman recalls about realizing that a group of boys had surrounded her in a bedroom after she had passed out at a house party, "as I didn't want to make it awkward for some stupid reason."

The story that girls are taught to adopt, as Febos puts it, is not a logical one. To internalize it requires a lifetime of careful conditioning, and an absence of anyone trying to counter it. I graduated 20 years ago, but as far as I can tell, the culture I remember remains intact without a corrective—only now those who have been conditioned to abuse have more tools with which to do so. When I was 16 (*puts on senior voice*), texting was still so new that you had to request it as an upgrade; not one week after I did, some friends of my first boyfriend, an arrogant kid on the hockey team, sent me a string of misspelled messages calling me a frigid bitch for not sleeping with him, and detailing exactly how far he'd gone with a different girl to get what they saw as his due. If they could have, I'm sure they would have sent proof. A decade later, when my sister was attending the school, she told me that nudes and revenge porn had infested its culture as silently and damagingly as moths colonize a closet. Misogyny will always occupy any space it's given. Expecting girls to be able to stanch its creep by themselves is too much.

To be a girl is to be perfectly vulnerable to predation: sexual, emotional, and even intellectual. It isn't just one school—a slew of others in the UK, including Westminster and St. Paul's Boys, have begun addressing charges that current and former students have raised in recent weeks, while in the US, prep schools including Horace Mann and Thacher have faced their own reckonings by students alleging decades of abuse. And to be clear, a culture of institutionalized misogyny also puts queer people in danger, and people of color especially so; the Dulwich document contains a whole section on how the alleged "discriminatory worldview" of certain students encouraged homophobic abuse and racialized violence. A substantial 2017 study by the Georgetown Law Center on Poverty and Inequality found that Black girls are significantly more likely to be seen as more adult-like and less innocent than their white peers, particularly between the ages of five and 14. Black girls in that age group are widely presumed to know more about sex, and to need less comforting, nurturing, and protection. The authors concluded that this kind of "adultification" of those girls "is a form of dehumanization, robbing Black children of the very essence of what makes childhood distinct." Black girls are barely even allowed to be girls at all.

In the absence of specific lessons that emphasize self-worth and autonomy, internalizing the things some boys say they're entitled to becomes disturbingly easy. As teenagers, we were taught how to put condoms on bananas, but not how to ask boys to wear them. We were taught trigonometry and Catullus and the history of feminism, but not how to apply the idea that we are equal human beings to social situations in which we are seen as prey. We were also taught to prickle with shame for being frigid, or being easy—a taxonomy so reductively designed that it leaves little room to simply exist. For decades, Febos notes in her introduction, "I considered it impossible to undo most of this indoctrination. Knowing about it was not enough. But I have found its undoing more possible than I expected."

PROGRESS, THOREAU WROTE, IS when we "unlearn and learn anew what we thought we knew before," which is likely the most insight Thoreau ever had into the hostile state of female adolescence. Unlearning is what *Girlhood* is all about. Febos is a memoirist whose previous books, *Abandon Me* and *Whip Smart*, laid bare her history as a professional dominatrix, a writer, and a heroin addict. *Girlhood*, though, struck me as more of a treatise. It's disquisitive and catalytic—it doesn't demand change so much as expose certain injustices so starkly that you might feel you cannot abide them another minute.

When Febos was 11, a girl growing up on Cape Cod, her body began to change. "Before puberty," she writes, "I moved through the world and toward other people without hesitance or self-consciousness." But the metamorphosis of her physical self changed the way the world related to her. Her mother bought her a book, *The What's Happening to My Body? Book for Girls*, which explained the hormonal changes but not, Febos writes, "why grown men in passing cars, to whom I had always been happily invisible, now leered at me." Or why an older boy at her bus stop now repeatedly chased and spat at her, or why a 25-year-old man followed her into a bathroom. That event became a story passed around by Febos's friends, one eventually reclaimed by Febos. In hindsight, Febos is an obvious victim, a child devoid of power. In her friends' reading at the time, her new physicality was responsible for what happened, and something for which she deserved to be shamed. The scene exposes how insidiously childhood logic twists events into a kind of poisonous pretzel, infinite and self-perpetuating.

This upside-down logic pervades the accounts of things Dulwich College boys are alleged to have done. At 13, one girl recalls, she went to a party with boys who encouraged the girls to take shots, even though they'd rarely had alcohol before. "Soon I was being pressured and essentially forced into giving one of them a blow job with my friend," she writes. "We both reflect on this in horror now but at the time were labelled slags and felt we deserved it." There is, and always has been, a trap within the bafflingly short virgin–whore continuum: Girls are shamed into doing things they don't want to do and then shamed for doing them. Another girl, too drunk to consent to sex with the boy she says raped her, recalls how she later overheard him excoriating her to his friends for being too lazy to get on top. When I read this, I thought about the first season of

Game of Thrones, and how Daenerys Targaryen compels her rapist to be nicer to her by essentially putting on a more exciting performance when he rapes her.

Untangling the lessons of girlhood from the cultural works that teach them to us is impossible; they are often our most committed teachers. Febos lucidly scrutinizes the movies that taught women to accept stalking as a gesture of devotion. In 2004, when she was in her 20s and living in Brooklyn, she was reading one night when she heard a male voice outside her bedroom window. "Pretty girl," the voice said. "You touching yourself?" She froze; she pulsed with terror; she realized he couldn't actually see through the window shade, which was drawn. That meant he'd been watching her long enough to know who she was. She wondered what she might have done in the past to catch his attention. "How brazenly uncareful I had been to stand naked in my own bed-room," she thinks. "We all know," Febos writes, with irony, "the ways women invite their victimization by walking after dark, wearing short skirts, or having big breasts. The pathology of victimhood would also claim that self-blaming and shame were my very ordinary attempt to explain what had happened to me, to assert control over it by assuming responsibility."

But then she thinks about Brian De Palma's movie *Body Double*. The homage to *Rear Window* and *Vertigo* is about a man who begins watching a woman who dances every night in front of her window wearing only panties. This voyeuristic act is presented not as a violation but as an appropriate response to a woman who is clearly performing. This kind of narrative, absurdly common in popular culture, exonerates men, Febos writes: "If we want it, where is the crime?" She flits through some of the stories that have reinforced this pernicious myth: *Revenge of the Nerds*, *American Beauty*, *Animal House*, *Porky's*, *The Girl Next Door*. "What a powerful message it is," Febos continues, "that your body ought to be available to any man passing by. It will only inconvenience you to protest. Better to tolerate it. Reframe it as nothing memorable, as a joke, as journalism, as privilege, even as a precursor to love."

What is a demand for nudes if not an enforcement of the belief that women are supposed to perform for male pleasure, and even to want to do so? One girl in the Dulwich College document recalls how, while she was having sex with a boy, she turned around and saw that he was filming her without her permission. "I started crying and felt even more uncomfortable and scared that he had that power of the video over me," she writes. Another girl remembers being filmed without her consent in a compromising position at a party, and the resulting videos being posted all over social media. "Since then," she writes, "I have been incredibly paranoid in any kind of intimate situation or party, I feel as though I can't enjoy myself without the fear of being watched or ridiculed."

WHEN I WAS THINKING about this story, I asked my sister whether she remembered receiving any meaningful education about consent as a teen; she said she didn't, and asked her friend's sister, who graduated high school three years ago and remembered a single video with no follow-up discussion. (In spring 2021, petitions started circulating in the United Kingdom demanding that the government build into the national curriculum better education on consent, sexual violence, and harassment.) One bizarre lesson my sister did recall involved policemen coming to school to teach internet safety. The assembled girls were told to imagine that they were chatting online with "Nadia," a supposed peer, only to have an adult man surprise them from behind a door at the back of the auditorium, saying menacingly that *he* was Nadia. When I heard this, I couldn't stop laughing. It's exactly the kind of slapstick, quaintly uncool scenario that cops would dream up to terrify teenage girls, and that teenage girls would entirely ignore. Not trusting the Nadias you've never met is, mostly, obvious. Not trusting the people you know, the ones you've grown up with, is much harder. To do so is to reject your own instincts, your entire history of being.

School is where you learn what you are worth. Not your actual value as a human being, which is a much more complicated blend of the person you're trying to be and how you treat others, but your social worth, an arbitrary appraisal by others that's inherently flawed and yet hard to shake, even in adulthood. It's a construction, and a trap. Febos refers to Foucault's panopticon, Laura Mulvey's idea of the male gaze, and John Berger's *Ways of Seeing* as she analyzes how women are constantly surveyed in the world—how, often, their response is to begin surveying themselves through the same defective lens, and to find themselves unworthy. This kind of self-scrutiny, Febos writes, "is an integral part of the mechanism that induced my own bifurcated self-image at eleven years old, at fourteen, at twenty-three."

Enough, we should say. Male pleasure is not paramount. Boys do not get to keep shaming and bullying girls into doing things they don't want to do. Boys should *want* not to do this. Not incapacitating girls until they're beyond refusal or blackmailing them into sending nudes should be a point of pride. And girls should learn to resist those who propagate the lie, as Febos writes, that "women's bodies are inherently defective, aesthetically defective . . . We are too short, too tall, too fat, too thin, too dark, too stiff, too loose, too solicitous, too yielding, too assertive, too weak, or too strong." We should question why, as Febos puts it with bracing simplicity, "both men and women prioritize the comfort and wellbeing of men over women's safety, comfort, even the truth of their bodily experience."

To do all this isn't easy. The established, false metrics of self-worth are insidious and serpentine. Jumping out of a door in an auditorium is easier than explaining the nuances of consent and self-love. But changing the lessons of adolescence is important. I never once needed trigonometry and I couldn't find Catullus in a crossword these days, but Febos's education is a kind I surely could have used.

A

THE BALLAD OF
TAYSTEE JEFFERSON

July 2019

IN THE VERY FIRST SCENE of the very first episode of *Orange Is the New Black*, released on Netflix in 2013, Piper (played by Taylor Schilling) takes her first shower as an inmate at Litchfield prison. As she shivers under trickles of lukewarm water, her reverie is interrupted by a loudspeaker announcement about mandatory lice checks, and by Tasha "Taystee" Jefferson (Danielle Brooks), who arrives in her nightgown and demands that Piper hurry up. The two women banter for a moment about Piper's paper-towel shower sandals and her "TV titties." As Piper walks away, the camera lets her go and instead closes in on Taystee, who's singing loudly and joyfully in the stall.

The scene seems to encapsulate something, now: Piper was always ostensibly the central character of Jenji Kohan's prison-set dramedy, but Piper's genial vacuousness as a heroine was set up from the beginning as a backdrop against which other characters could sing. And as *Orange Is the New Black* continued over seven seasons, the woman who became the true core of the series was Taystee. In the script, she was a foil for Piper that the writers could use to explore the school-to-prison pipeline in America. Whereas Piper grew up in affluence and studied comparative literature at Smith, Taystee was raised in group homes and foster care, and first went to juvenile prison at the age of 16. Piper traveled after college and made artisanal soaps; Taystee worked in fast-food restaurants. Piper was lured into smuggling cash for a drug dealer because the thrill of it excited her; Taystee wanted no part in the drug trade, but ended up doing the books for a dealer who offered her an alternative to yet another group home.

By Season 2, when *Orange* got to more aggressively deconstructing its Trojan-horse setup, Taystee was already being positioned as the show's most crucial component. Through her story, the series considered the failures of the parole system, recidivism, and—in later seasons—the way racist institutions configure and protect themselves. But she was also, thanks to Brooks's performance, one of the most spectacular characters on television. Resourceful, sharp, outlandish, funny, and perpetually kind, Taystee continued to thwart all the ways in which the system tried to beat her down. In Season 6, she and Piper had a scene that skewered Piper's privilege in a single exchange. "What is it about me that makes people want to fuck with me?" a disconsolate Piper asked, having had pink gum lodged in her hair and drugs planted in her shoe.

"Can I be real with you?" Taystee responded. "It's 'cause of what they see when they look at you. They don't see you. They see the shit they never had. Money, education, opportunity. That's why they never gonna stop fucking with you, because of what you represent. But at least that's only in here. People out there been fucking with me my entire fucking life. They see dangerous, poor, ghetto Black girl that should be locked up in here forever. So, like, if you want to trade places, I'm game."

"How do you deal with it?" Piper replied, chastened.

"I try to survive," Taystee said.

REALISTICALLY, PIPER WAS ALWAYS going to get out of prison. The show spun out her 15-month sentence for as long as it could, given the creep of jail time and the inevitability of aging, even for TV actors. There were moments when it seemed like she might be headed for extra time, a Sisyphean ordeal of a sentence that just kept increasing. But a woman of her means, with her support network and her lawyers, wasn't destined to get trapped in the carceral system. *Orange*'s final season documents some of the struggles Piper experiences in the outside world: the indignity of menial jobs, the mounting bills imposed by mandatory drug tests and parole checks, the dismay of living in her brother's guest bedroom in Jackson Heights and having to witness her sister-in-law's arduous regimen of "elimination communication" potty training.

The final flashback of the show's run, though, makes clear how easy Piper has it. In the 12th episode of Season 7,

"The Big House," *Orange* jumps back in time to when Taystee was released from Litchfield in Season 1. As she arrives home from her job at KFC, she finds out that the woman she's staying with is being evicted, and she has to choose between homelessness and staying with a friend's cousin who'll put her to work selling drugs. As Taystee tries to decide what to do, she gets a call from Poussey, who tells her that pain and upheaval are only temporary. But the sound of her friend's voice is enough to convince Taystee that she was better off inside, with a place to sleep, food to eat, and people who loved her. It's a split-second decision that sparks a chain of events that will threaten her life.

Piper's position at the very end of *Orange Is the New Black* was predetermined. Taystee's represented a choice on the part of the writers. No show of the current era has so sharply used juxtaposition to depict inequality in America. From its earliest episodes, *Orange* has used the art of contiguity—placing certain scenes next to each other—to make explicit points. In the series finale, "Here's Where We Get Off," Kohan (who wrote the episode) follows a scene of Piper's father discussing his attempts to "Marie Kondo" his possessions with a sequence of a homeless camp being razed. As its inhabitants race to collect their most precious possessions, one man looks back wistfully at an abandoned couch, as if he's thanking it for its service and letting it go. By pairing these two scenes, Kohan offers some withering insight into the privilege of clutter.

Taystee, similarly, has always stood next to Piper to illustrate what a white, blond, Smith-educated woman can't. And Taystee's fate over the final two seasons of the show has essentially represented *Orange*'s worldview. At the end of Season 4, after Poussey was killed when a guard suffocated her, a grieving Taystee incited a prison riot after realizing that the system would never bring her friend justice. Poussey's death, and the events that followed, cemented a shift in tone for the series, and a turn away from zanier plot developments toward pivotal questions of institutionalized racism and powerlessness. At the heart of them all was Taystee, who tried to negotiate an end to the riot, but was thwarted when Maria decided to release hostages to try to shave time off her own sentence. After armed responders forcibly entered the prison, they accidentally shot the sadistic captain of the guards, Desi Piscatella, and covered up his death, implicating Taystee. At the end of Season 6, she was convicted of murder.

Everything Taystee had previously told Piper was shown to be true. The jury in the courtroom didn't see *her*—her sense of humor, her intelligence, her potential, her empathy. They saw, instead, a Black woman in prison for dealing drugs, which was all they needed to see to believe she could also be a murderer. In dealing Taystee such a brutal hand, the writers on *Orange* gave the series its darkest story line since the death of Poussey. And they set up a conundrum for the show's final season. If they gave Taystee a happy ending and got her conviction thrown out, the series would sacrifice its commitment to accurately portraying the state of the justice system for so many of the unfairly incarcerated. But if they left her in despair, they'd be doing a disservice to a character who represented the show's heart.

In Season 7, Taystee's story got even darker. She tried to hang herself from a prison bunk, in a crushingly bleak scene, and when that failed, she asked Daya for drugs to help her end her own life. She wrote a letter to Cindy's daughter revealing her parentage, which indirectly led to Cindy's homelessness. And yet, as the season continued, Taystee kept finding fragments of things to cling to. Her friendship with Tamika, now Litchfield's warden, was one. Her realization that she could help other inmates get their GEDs by tutoring them was another. She came up with an idea for helping recently paroled women succeed on the outside by teaching them financial literacy and giving them microloans, via a fund named after Poussey. After she learned that her lawyer didn't think there was sufficient new evidence to open an appeal in her case, and Taystee realized all over again that she would likely be in prison for the rest of her life, she also found out that several inmates had passed their GED test. "You made this

A

happen," Tamika told her in a note. "Tomorrow will be better."

Will it? With Taystee, the show found an ending that wasn't uplifting, necessarily, but that wasn't outright devastating either. She remained unjustly incarcerated for murder, while the people who covered up Piscatella's death went free. Her friend was fired as the prison warden and replaced with an abusive, power-hungry, drug-smuggling guard. Still, Taystee was left with something to wake up for every day—the ability to help other women so that they'd have a better chance at life than she did. It's not the ending I wanted for her. It's not the ending she deserved. But it was a way for the show to reconcile its commitment to capturing the reality of the penal system with its duty to a character who helped carry it for seven seasons. Taystee didn't get justice, yet. (I'm still hopeful for a future version of the show in which she does.) But she did, despite everything, manage to survive.

II

TOLD

MAKING PEACE WITH JANE AUSTEN'S MARRIAGE PLOTS

July 2017

ALL SIX OF JANE AUSTEN'S novels end with weddings. On the final page of *Northanger Abbey*, readers are informed that "Henry and Catherine were married, the bells rang, and everybody smiled." *Sense and Sensibility* concludes with a twofer: Elinor and Edward are married "in Barton church early in the autumn," and Marianne is "placed in a new home" with Colonel Brandon. *Pride and Prejudice*'s Mrs. Bennet gets "rid of her two most deserving daughters" on the same day. *Mansfield Park* ends with Fanny and Edmund married, and their happiness "as secure as earthly happiness can be." In *Emma*, the titular character and Mr. Knightley are wed with "no taste for finery or parade," but with "perfect happiness" in their union. Anne Elliot, "tenderness itself," is married to Captain Wentworth in the last chapter of *Persuasion*, with only the prospect of war casting a shadow over her contentment.

The wide-ranging influence of Austen's marriage plots is hard to quantify. Nor is it entirely her fault. When Carrie marries Mr. Big at the end of *Sex and the City*, not with a bang but a City Hall whimper, the "happily-ever-after" conclusion is as much a nod to the conventions of fairy tales (the shoe fits) as it is to Austen's satirical romances. And yet there are few other authors who've so reliably concluded stories about women with accounts of their marriages. Austen's weddings mark a natural endpoint, offering finite resolution (marriage in 19th-century England was almost entirely irreversible) and domestic and financial security for her heroines. They also set a standard for romantic comedies that's been impossibly pervasive: Women's stories end, definitively, with marriage.

For me at least, this has long been a source of some irritation. Marriage plots, satisfying as they are, only offer a tiny window into a woman's life, and they imply that getting married is easily the most significant thing she will ever do. They zero in on the "before" at the expense of the "after." (Fan fiction alone will testify to the rampant curiosity about the state of Elizabeth and Darcy's marriage, and not just in the bedroom.) They also lead to culture focusing predominantly on younger women. Even in Austen's work, the scholar Judith Lowder Newton has written, "marriage demands resignation even as it prompts rejoicing, initiates new life while it confirms a flickering suspicion that the best is over."

Austen's six novels achieved varying commercial success throughout her life, but their impact on storytelling in Western culture has been profound. Every time a rom-com ends with an engagement, or a wedding, or even a counterintuitive promise to be *unmarried* to someone for the rest of their life (*Four Weddings and a Funeral*), their influence feels palpable. Loving Austen unequivocally, then, means coming to terms with the paradox at the heart of her work: No one did more to challenge the conventions and strictures of marriage for women in the 19th century, while simultaneously enshrining it as the ultimate happy ending for her worthy, intelligent, and independent characters.

Jane Austen was born in 1775, toward the end of the 18th century, a period that saw the forceful emergence of an English middle class. Men who hadn't inherited land could seek prosperity as businessmen or clergymen, or as officers in the army and navy (Captain Wentworth, in *Persuasion*, returns a wealthy man from the Napoleonic Wars thanks to money he earned by capturing enemy ships). But the flip side of a shifting economy, as the historian Kirstin Olsen notes, was "the gradual disappearance of respectable work for middle-class women." Women were barred from becoming lawyers, doctors, politicians, or judges, which left them, Olsen writes, "with not occupations but hobbies: music, drawing, needlework, and artistic or social patronage."

Austen's sense of frustration about this enforced and unequal uselessness is detectable even in her earlier works. *Sense and Sensibility*, which she started working on before 1796, begins with three daughters plunged into poverty when their father dies and their brother inherits the family estate. At the time, the only means women had of bettering themselves was marriage. Austen's novels follow the structural model of romances and fairy tales, where circumstances and complications keep a couple from their inevitable union. But they also consistently refer to the economic realities of marriage for women, which none of her characters can afford to ignore. In *Pride and Prejudice*, Austen wryly introduces Mr. Darcy by writing that "he soon drew the attention of the room by his fine, tall person, handsome features, noble mien, and the report which was in general circulation within five minutes after his entrance of his having ten thousand a year."

This tension between naively interpreting marriage as a love match and cynically calculating its potential profits is embodied in *Pride and Prejudice* by two very different characters. Lydia Bennet pursues men thoughtlessly and wantonly, without regard to their economic situation or their potential as providers. Charlotte Lucas, by contrast, marries Mr. Collins, a buffoon, purely for financial security, horrifying her friend Elizabeth in the process. "Without thinking highly either of men or matrimony," Austen writes of Charlotte, "marriage had always been her object; it was the only provision for well-educated young women of small fortune, and however uncertain of giving happiness, must be their pleasantest preservative from want."

Elizabeth, by contrast to both Charlotte and Lydia, is Austen's attempt to reconcile two different imperatives—to prove that marriage can be both a true love match between two compatible people and a means of significant economic improvement for women. Austen, the scholar Karen Newman writes, "exposes the fundamental discrepancy in her society between its avowed ideology of love and its implicit economic motivation." The very first sentence of *Pride and Prejudice* is a wink; a statement that single men in possession of good fortunes *must* be in want of a wife, when all of Austen's readers know the opposite to be true—single women with no fortune or means to speak of are very much in need of husbands. As Henry Tilney, Catherine's love interest, states in *Northanger Abbey*, "Man has the advantage of choice; woman only the power of refusal."

This reality makes marriage not just an objective but a business that otherwise unoccupied women can devote significant time to. The first third of *Pride and Prejudice*, Lowder Newton notes, "consists of very little but women talking or thinking or scheming about men." In *Sense and Sensibility*, Mrs. Jennings, an independently wealthy woman whose daughters are married, devotes herself to making matches for other young women in a kind of self-appointed act of community service. In *Emma*, Emma Woodhouse is a rich young woman who has no need to get married, but she also takes to matchmaking with enthusiastic and misguided gusto, causing chaos with her lack of regard to the realities of social classes.

The reason why Austen, who never married, leads all her characters to the altar in concluding their stories is relatively simple. Narrative conventions in comedy require happy endings. Austen obeyed the rigid strictures of the marriage plot, but she also subversively forced her readers to see the awkward reality of marriage for women. Some critics argue that she doesn't go far enough in challenging it as an institution: In *Pride and Prejudice*, Lowder Newton argues, "Elizabeth's . . . untraditional power is rewarded not with some different life but with woman's traditional life, with love and marriage." Others, like William H. Magee, counter that Austen reworked the marriage plot to suit her own agenda. "By doing so," he writes, "she made the convention a vital feature of her own art and developed it into a criticism of the life allotted by her society to young women of the times."

TWO HUNDRED YEARS AFTER her death, Austen's marriage plots remain very much a part of the cultural framework. "Ever since the days of Jane Austen," Koa Beck wrote in *The Atlantic* in 2014, "pop-culture consumers have been drawn to stories about female protagonists who find 'happily ever after' in marriage and motherhood." The thriving genre of wedding movies, rather than exposing the contradictions at the heart of the institution of marriage, mocks the gargantuan business of planning a wedding, exposed in *Bride Wars*, and *27 Dresses*, and *The Wedding Planner*, and *The Wedding Singer*. Austen would surely approve.

But she might also question why so many works of popular culture haven't done more to expand the boundaries of telling stories about women's lives. Worldwide, the second highest-grossing film of 2017 was *Beauty and the Beast*, an adaptation of a fairy tale written to prepare young French girls for arranged marriages. As a novelist, Austen was keenly attuned to culture's powers of persuasion. In *Northanger Abbey*, Catherine Morland is almost brought to disaster by all the Gothic novels she reads, which lead her to interpret ordinary events as sensational and supernatural.

For me, making peace with Austen's marriage plots, and the many, many imitators they sparked, means considering the fact that she overestimated her audience. She used the rituals of romantic comedy to expose what marriage really meant for women who had no other means of economic improvement, hoping that we'd see the injustice of it. She gave her heroines a kind of power and agency that she herself lacked. "When Austen allows Elizabeth to express critical attitudes," Lowder Newton writes, "to act upon them without penalty, when she endows Elizabeth with the power to alter her lot, Austen is moving against traditional notions of feminine behavior and feminine fate."

What contemporary culture took from her novels, though, is that stories about complex, intriguing women should end in marriage, however improbably. It's the moral of *The Philadelphia Story*, and *Gentlemen Prefer Blondes*, and *While You Were Sleeping*, and *The Princess Diaries 2. Clueless*, an adaptation of *Emma*, nods to the rule by wrapping up with a wedding fakeout—it isn't Cher who's getting married, but her homely teacher Miss Geist. Concluding with a wedding implies that all involved live happily ever after, something even Austen knew was unlikely. Her ending to *Mansfield Park*, in which the happiness of Fanny and Edmund is "as secure as earthly happiness can be," includes an ironic tip of the hat to readers who know by experience that earthly happiness is rarely as reliable as storytellers would have it.

THE SOFT RADICALISM
OF EROTIC FICTION

June 2021

PLEASURE, IN THE NOVELS OF Jackie Collins, tends to be abundant but hard-earned—imagine Pandora, having opened the box containing every sin plaguing humanity, retiring to a beach house in Malibu with two Weimaraners and a finely muscled masseur. The titles of her later books nod to desire and its cost: *Lethal Seduction*, *Deadly Embrace*, *Dangerous Kiss*. And in life, the British-born author emanated a similar combination of tough glamour. If I close my eyes, I can see the jacket photo on the glossy hardcovers in my childhood bedroom: Collins, standing in front of a blandly wealthy backdrop, her hair as rich as chocolate and her shoulders padded past the point of no return. These conspicuous displays of accomplishment read to me now as karmic winks at all the critics who disdained her. *Carry on with your carping, suckers*, she seems to say with her eyes, the light glinting off her abundant jewelry. *This pool is paid for*.

I have loved Jackie Collins since I was 11, when a friend pulled me into her parents' study in a drafty house in the English countryside to show me a particularly raunchy scene she'd found in her mother's copy of *Hollywood Kids*. After that, I was totally in thrall. From the late '60s—when she published her first book, *The World Is Full of Married Men*—until her death in 2015, Collins published 32 best-selling novels, characterized by their ballsy female characters, explicit bedroom scenes, and trenchant portrayals of the entertainment industry and its abuses of power. To read a Collins novel, as roughly half a billion of us humans have, is to know that sex and power are inextricable. No one mined the dynamics of both as astutely in the late 20th century as she did. (As she told *The New York Times* in 2007, "I published my first novel in 1968, when no one was writing about sex except Philip Roth.")

Collins's reputation, though, has always suffered from an instinctive tendency among her critics to be alarmed by what she sold: stories about empowered women seeking out gratification on their own terms. I didn't realize, until I watched the documentarian Laura Fairrie's *Lady Boss: The Jackie Collins Story*, quite how precipitously Collins tilted the curve of popular eroticism away from blushing maidens and crinoline toward Alaïa-clad entrepreneurs. As one interviewee in the film phrases it, Collins put "female sexuality at the center of the world, and people lost their minds." During the '70s and '80s, few authors were hotter: Collins made significant amounts of money; she shrugged off the shadow of her famous and pulchritudinous older sister, Joan; she socialized with the starriest of Los Angeles's British imports. And yet she seems to have been stung throughout her life by the rancor of her detractors. In one archival scene shot poolside during a party, the writer speaks earnestly about her plans for the day while the actor Roger Moore mimics the physique of a large-breasted woman behind her for the camera—a reminder that, even for her friends, she tended to be reduced to a smutty punch line.

Fairrie seems to have loved Collins too. *Lady Boss* is piercing, snappy, and seemingly devoted to its subject, whose personal archives provide a trove of insight. When Collins died in 2015, at the age of 77, she left a mass of documents—photograph albums, diaries, videos—due to the fact that she had been working on an autobiography that she never got to finish. The details are candid (Collins, at 15, had what she described as an affair with the 29-year-old Marlon Brando, who she writes called her "sincere, sweet, and luscious") and revelatory. Before Collins was 30, she lost her mother to cancer and her first husband, who experienced addiction and manic depression, to suicide. She also had an inferiority complex regarding her sister, whom she tried to follow into acting, after getting substantial plastic surgery. "I look awful," she writes in one desolate diary entry from the 1950s. "Joan told me so."

But Jackie's failed acting career gave her an unexpected gift. If she wasn't embraced into the capacious bosom of

Hollywood, she could scrutinize it quietly from the sidelines. Friend after friend tells Fairrie how Collins would go to parties, observing people, asking endless questions, and mentally storing notes for her next book. Her critiques of an industry riven equally with sleaze and aspiration are more incisive than she's given credit for: Decades before #MeToo, she was a thoughtful chronicler of the scourge of the casting couch, and the challenges that women behind the scenes faced in being taken seriously. *Hollywood Wives*, Collins's best-selling novel to date, skewers the quirks and toxicity of the moviemaking business—the pandering to male ego, the fragility of stardom, the ineffable taxonomy of who's hot and who's not. Her books are laden with hot male actors preying on underage girls and poisonous hustlers operating up and down the social ladder.

But her female characters tend to be bold, smart, and resilient. Lucky Santangelo, her most storied character—who *Lady Boss* theorizes is Collins's alter ego—overcomes a forced marriage, mob violence, a sexist father, and a litany of abuses to become a casino boss and the head of her own movie studio. Her message for readers, Collins told *The Los Angeles Times* in 1988, was that "women need to be stronger . . . Women have always been pushed into positions in the bedroom, the kitchen, the workforce. Women can do *anything*." It's easy to satirize her style, with its rampant descriptors ("Lucky was a slender,

A

long-limbed woman with an abundance of shoulder-length jet curls; dangerous black opal eyes; full, sensual lips; and a deep olive skin") and husky excess. But the substance beneath it merits closer attention. Collins's agent, Morton Janklow, argues in the film that "the great storyteller is rarer than the great writer, and Jackie was a great storyteller."

Fairrie includes clips from TV talk shows to underscore how gleefully Collins was torn apart, often to her face. The writer Clive James derides her work as vacant airport trash; the romance novelist Barbara Cartland tells Collins during one shared appearance that she thinks her books are "evil," to which Collins can only laugh. One talk-show appearance seems almost like an ambush: Audience members gathered by the British host Robert Kilroy-Silk lash out at Collins's supposedly fake feminism and "disgusting" morals while she watches, completely stunned. The comedians Dawn French and Jennifer Saunders gently parodied the saga of Jackie and Joan—rivalry, fame, and lots and lots of leopard print—in a legendary sketch titled "Lucky Bitches."

Male authors of potboilers have not historically received this treatment. Harold Robbins is still lauded as "the Onassis of supermarket literature"; Lee Child gets interviewed by *The New Yorker*'s David Remnick. But Collins's influence endures in other ways. For decades, the teenagers and women who read her novels heard over and over that they counted, that their pleasure and autonomy were as important as anyone else's. It's not an easy message to internalize, even now. *Lady Boss* makes me cherish Collins more than ever for her career-long commitment to delivering it.

THE REMARKABLE RISE OF
THE FEMINIST DYSTOPIA

October 2018

"EVER SINCE LAST WEEK," CEDAR explains on the first page of Louise Erdrich's 2017 book, *Future Home of the Living God*, "things have changed. Apparently—I mean, nobody knows—our world is running backward. Or forward. Or maybe sideways, in a way as yet ungrasped."

This passage has returned to me again and again in recent weeks, almost two years into the 45th presidency. It's never felt more obvious that something is very wrong with the shape and trajectory of the world, that time itself is out of joint. Perhaps you felt a similar sense of disorientation recently, watching one brave, intelligent, persuasive woman after another publicly rake through a traumatic moment in her life. Perhaps you felt, like I did, that something you'd previously felt safe taking for granted—that a man credibly accused of sexual assault might not be elevated to a position of profound power over women—was no longer something to trust.

Maybe you watched the American president openly mock the testimony of a woman who says she was assaulted. Perhaps you thought about sexual assault—your own, or the ones you know have happened to your friends, your family members. Maybe you'd assumed until now that the world could only be improved; that each generation would get stronger, kinder, and wiser; that women would eventually teach men not to hurt them. You saw progress eking out its path: women listened to, men sent to prison. But then things began to change. And you observed, as Cedar does, that the world feels like it's running backward. Or sideways. Or in some direction that makes no sense at all.

This feels like a particularly strange moment in history, but it's one that writers seem to have anticipated: The past two years have seen a spate of works delving into the discombobulation of the present. During the early days of the Trump administration, readers sought out dystopian stories that connected the turbulence and the racism and the alternative facts of the 45th presidency with anxieties the world has had before. Over the last couple of years, though, fiction's dystopias have changed. They're largely written by, and concerned with, women. Picking up a mantle passed down by writers such as Octavia Butler, they imagine worlds ravaged by climate change, worlds in which humanity's progress unravels. Most significantly, they consider reproduction, and what happens when societies try to legislate it.

Some of these novels imagine preposterous scenarios, like women being shocked by Fitbit-like bracelets if they

A

utter more than 100 words a day, or women evolving until they develop the power to physically hurt men at will. But some aren't preposterous at all, and that's where it gets more alarming. Writers including Erdrich, Naomi Alderman, and Bina Shah are warning readers of what could happen in a near-future world, with sperm counts mysteriously plummeting, global temperatures and STD rates rising, and a pivotal anti-abortion vote poised to tip the balance of the Supreme Court. Dystopian fiction isn't soothing anymore. It's too close for comfort.

THE NOVEL THAT'S RECEIVED the most attention over the past two years from women readers troubled by the news actually arrived smack in the middle of the Reagan administration. In 1985, as America lurched socially to the right in what was seen as a rebuke of the sexual revolution, Margaret Atwood published *The Handmaid's Tale*, a speculative vision of a repressive theocratic state in America enabled by mass infertility and nuclear fallout.

Decades later, when readers returned to the book in the wake of Trump's election (and as a TV adaptation debuted on Hulu), it didn't matter that the book's most lurid imaginings (state-sanctioned rapes ripped from the Bible, sexual and reproductive slavery for the few remaining fertile women) weren't close to what was happening in a contemporary American reality. The book resonated so acutely because many younger women who'd grown up mostly assuming that things could only get better for gender equality were seeing hard proof of the opposite.

There were moments when life seemed to be doing its utmost to imitate Atwood's novel. When Oklahoma lawmakers tried to pass a bill requiring women to get written permission from their sexual partner before having abortions. When the Trump administration sanctioned children and babies being literally ripped from their parents' arms, and when the White House Press Secretary Sarah Huckabee Sanders claimed that the policy of family separation was actually "very biblical" because it was enforcing existing laws.

But for the most part, women connected with *The Handmaid's Tale* in this moment because the path of history seemed to be suddenly pointing the wrong way. That's why protesters in white bonnets and crimson gowns have become the uncanny visual motif of women demonstrating in the Trump era. (Not to mention the fact that the president, a man who seemed to characterize himself as having been open to the possibility of terminating a girlfriend's pregnancy in the past, now feels compelled to outlaw abortion altogether via his nomination of conservative, anti-abortion justices to the Supreme Court.)

Many of the recent speculative-fiction books by women have drawn inspiration from *The Handmaid's Tale*, or at least its model for how Gilead might come to pass. Shah's 2018 novel, *Before She Sleeps*, is set in a near-future Middle

A

Eastern city, in a world that's been similarly decimated by nuclear war and disease (in this case, a strain of HPV that kills infected women within months). Surviving fertile women are forced into polygamous marriages with multiple men. In Erdrich's *Future Home of the Living God*, society breaks down after women start bearing children with birth defects, babies that seem to resemble earlier species of humankind. The government declares a state of emergency, martial law is installed, and pregnant women are quickly forced into state custody.

Of all the potential precipitating factors for totalitarian government, women writers have always found intriguing terrain in infertility. The prospective end of humanity is calamitous enough to imagine drastic ends being justified. And men have proved themselves so willing over millennia to demand total control over what women do with their bodies that the prospect of them going to extreme measures is more than conceivable. (In September 2018, the former Trump administration staffer Jason Miller was accused of putting an abortifacient in his mistress's drink without her knowledge—a plot so dystopian that it was featured in a recent episode of *Black Mirror*.)

The theme of infertility charged *The Handmaid's Tale*, and P. D. James's 1992 novel, *Children of Men*, set in the then-terrifying future of 2021 amid collapsing global birth rates. Then there was Hillary Jordan's 2011 novel,

When She Woke, which also imagines an STD epidemic leaving most people infertile (one consequence of which is that *Roe v. Wade* is overturned). Erdrich first began working on *Future Home of the Living God* in 2002, when—during the buildup to the 2003 U.S. invasion of Iraq—she felt that progress was reversing. She picked up the novel again in 2016, when "photographs of white men in dark suits deciding crucial issues of women's health" compelled her to believe that the issues it considered were more urgent than ever.

In *Future Home of the Living God*, Cedar, the narrator, is a pregnant woman of American Indian heritage who was adopted by a white couple, and who seeks out her birth mother to try to learn more about her genetic history. As her pregnancy develops, she becomes more and more vulnerable: physically incapacitated by her changing body and targeted by a dictatorial state that's rounding up pregnant women. Cedar's pregnancy conveys how reproduction is often used in dystopian fiction—as a metaphor for a loss of control. It also alludes to the forced sterilizations of Native American, Black, and poor women by the U.S. government during the 1970s, likened by a chief tribal judge for the North Cheyenne Reservation at the time to a modern form of genocide.

But Erdrich also communicates Cedar's contradictory emotions when it comes to her baby. She's terrified by the state of the world around her: Climate change has made winters a thing of the past, and animals are evolving rapidly into strange, alarming forms. The prospect of mankind making its world unlivable is a potent theme in the novel, particularly in the context of recent news that the Trump administration predicts a seven-degree rise in global temperatures by the end of this century. Climate change isn't just an abstract element in dystopian fiction by women: It informs everything, particularly the subject of reproduction itself.

Still, Cedar is unpredictably thrilled by her pregnancy, and by the prospect of motherhood. Erdrich hits on the paradox of female fertility: The ability to reproduce is both a lifeline and a life sentence. As Moira Weigel wrote in a review of Hulu's *The Handmaid's Tale*, "The one thing that gives you value in society is the very thing for which you are hated."

ANXIETIES CAN BE METAPHORICAL in speculative fiction; they can also be blazingly literal. In *Parable of the Talents*, Octavia Butler's 1998 sequel to her germinal speculative work *Parable of the Sower*, women who speak their minds too forcefully are at risk of having their tongues cut out. (That novel also somehow featured a fundamentalist politician whose platform was to "Make America Great Again.") *Vox*, a 2018 novel by Christina Dalcher, seems to nod to Butler as it tries to imagine how men are taught to believe that women are second-class citizens. *Vox*'s premise is that a new conservative Christian government in the United States has banned women from speaking more than 100 words a day, in order to enforce male supremacy within every subsection of society. Women are fitted with high-tech bracelets that deliver electric shocks if they breach their limits (the shocks grow increasingly severe the more the women transgress).

The setup is at least a little ludicrous, and Dalcher never puts in real effort to imagine how such an egregious system might have been implemented. She's more interested in the silencing of women as an allegory. Dalcher began working on the book after rereading *The Handmaid's Tale* in 2017 and watching the women's marches after the Trump inauguration. Jean, her narrator, is a neurolinguist who was working on pioneering experiments regarding speech disorders until the new administration mandated that women stay home. Jean's frustration at being unable to voice her true, complex thoughts and feelings is palpable, and it strikes a chord with some of the disempowerment many women might currently feel. But *Vox*'s most interesting element is the way it tries to imagine how easily men could be compelled to deprive even the women they love of their basic rights.

Vox begins to lose potency once it shifts from a thoughtful account of Jean's reality to an action thriller. (The Hulu adaptation of *The Handmaid's Tale*, interestingly enough, suffered from the same faults in its second

A

season.) Shah's *Before She Sleeps* also shifts early on from a radical thought experiment about a repressive futuristic regime in the Middle East to a conventional romance, and thwarts its potential in the process. The question of how other countries might regress in the face of disease, infertility, or climate change is a fascinating one, given that so much speculative fiction by women is rooted in the U.S. and its own distinctive cultural anxieties and dark history. Erdrich, like Atwood before her, defines America as a country to be fled from, while Canada and Mexico remain progressive havens that are maddeningly out of reach.

THE CONVENTIONAL THINKING ON dystopian fiction is that it serves as both a comfort and a warning. Speculative stories point to how much worse things could be, but also how much worse they could get. They remind readers of the stunning breadth of human frailty. We see the world distorted, sometimes beyond recognition, and it prompts us to look at our own reality from different angles. *The Handmaid's Tale*, Margaret Atwood told me in 2017, is just a mashup of elements taken from different moments in history—she borrowed some of Gilead from a trip she took to Afghanistan in 1978, as well as from Nicolae Ceausescu's rule in Romania, when abortion and contraception were outlawed. Nothing was invented. Nothing was inconceivable, because everything had already happened in one country or another, the U.S. included.

But *The Power*, Naomi Alderman's striking 2017 novel, does something totally different. It turns the hierarchy of the world upside down and, in doing so, helps you see it in total clarity. Alderman's conceit is that women in an era much like this one suddenly develop a "skein," a strip of striated muscle that allows them to generate electricity at will. For the first time in history, women have the physical power to hurt, incapacitate, and kill men. "It doesn't matter that she shouldn't, that she never would," one character thinks. "What matters is that she could, if she wanted. The power to hurt is a kind of wealth."

The thing that viral Twitter threads and charts and testimonials have spent the past two years trying to communicate—the power differentials built into sexual assault—Alderman illuminates almost effortlessly. The genius of *The Power* is that it conveys how entirely the world is built on male power and male privilege, to the extent that societal structures topple as soon as women are given the advantage. In Riyadh, after two young girls are murdered by their uncles for practicing the power, women take to the streets by the thousands, while the male police forces are too afraid to arrest them. In Moldova, women who've been prisoners of sex traffickers are suddenly free. "The change has happened too fast for the men to learn the new tricks they need," Alderman writes. "It is a gift."

For the women in Alderman's book, gaining the power means realizing, almost for the first time, how powerless

A

they'd previously been. Allie, a teenager abused by her foster father, is able to fight back. She flees the house, pauses momentarily to wonder whether she should steal a knife to protect herself, and then "remembers—and the thought makes her laugh—that aside from cutting her dinner she really has no need for a knife, no need at all." When she hitchhikes, cars refuse to stop. The male drivers, she realizes, are afraid of her.

Alderman's world feels liberating. It's not meant to be. *The Power* is built around the argument that women are no less corruptible than men—that given the opportunity, they'd abuse physical power just as frequently. It's an opinion Alderman shares with Atwood, her mentor, who made clear in *The Handmaid's Tale* that there will always be women willing to hurt other women in exchange for a modicum of power of their own. Erdrich, too, writes female characters who commit egregious acts into *Future Home of the Living God*. "You have to ask, are women better than men?" Alderman told *The New York Times*. "They're not. People are people. You don't have to think that all men are horrible to know there are some men who abuse their strength. Why wouldn't the same hold true for women?"

Even so, what distinguishes *The Power* from other recent works is its thrilling view of a world so totally upended and so full of possibility, rather than a fictional universe that feels plausibly like a news broadcast from the future. The current spate of speculative works by and about women is surely a response to a present that itself feels grossly distorted. The process of examining how—and why—our own reality became so troubling is a valuable one, even if only for readers who were already compelled to undertake it. But being absorbed in a world, fleetingly, where women don't have to be afraid is more than a thought experiment. It's a profound, powerful relief.

III

CHOSEN

THE CALAMITY OF
UNWANTED MOTHERHOOD

—————

May 2022

THE PROTAGONIST OF PENELOPE MORTIMER's 1958 novel, *Daddy's Gone a-Hunting*, is a 37-year-old housewife named Ruth, who is sliding into a madness of midlife suffocation and despair. Alone in her kitchen early in the novel, Ruth drinks gin and tentatively confesses to an imagined listener the source of all her angst. When she married Rex, her trivial bully of a husband, at 18, she was three months pregnant with their daughter, Angela. "She doesn't know, of course," Ruth explains, to no one. "I didn't want to get married. I didn't want Angela. We had to get married. There was nothing else to do."

The burden of consequence on Ruth is a dead weight. She has no perceptible life force, no desires, less shape than crumpled tissue paper. Her fuzziness is countered in the novel by Mortimer's caustic narration, which laces Ruth's ennui with a ferocious current of social critique. *Daddy's Gone a-Hunting*, now being reissued in the U.S., was published several years before Betty Friedan's *The Feminine Mystique*. But the novel, seemingly set in the late '50s, appears to anticipate what Friedan proposed as "the problem that has no name"—the profound unhappiness of a generation of educated women trapped in the domestic sphere with no way out. In one chapter, Mortimer likens the women of "the Common," Ruth's suburban community, to icebergs, outwardly "bright and shining" but uniquely scratched up under the surface. "Some are happy," she writes, "some poisoned with boredom; some drink too much and some, below the demarcation line, are slightly crazy; some love their husbands and some are dying from lack of love; a few have talent, as useless to them as a dying limb." Together, "their energy could start a revolution, power half of Southern England, drive an atomic plant." Deprived of an outlet, however, it tends to short-circuit.

Ruth's despair is clearly rooted in her accidental pregnancy as a teenager, her necessary marriage to a man she despises, and her obligation to care for an unwanted child when she was still essentially a child herself. The novel's animating force is a simple, repetitive plot point: Her daughter, the now 18-year-old Angela, announces to Ruth that she's pregnant. Ruth becomes angry; she also finds, once again, that she's being forced by circumstance into acting against her will. "It wasn't that she had taken a step; she had been pushed, stumbling forward and finding responsibility thrust into her arms, finding herself committed without knowing how it had happened," Mortimer writes. Angela is intent on having her

A

pregnancy terminated, which was unlawful in the U.K. until 1968. To save her daughter from repeating history, Ruth has to balance conflicting impulses—her desire to protect Angela from the risk of an illegal procedure versus her desire to secure for her a future less miserable than her own.

Daddy's Gone a-Hunting is largely based on Mortimer's own experiences. Like Ruth, she was married at 19 and had her first child in short order; like Ruth, she helped her eldest daughter get an illegal abortion when she became pregnant while studying at a university. In a later, semi-autobiographical novel, *The Pumpkin Eater*, which explores marital infidelity and disaffection, Mortimer presented scenes of middle-class life with a remarkably acidic touch, stripping away any vestiges of illusion or pretense. With *Daddy's Gone a-Hunting*, she steps lightly into a sparse and immensely tricky genre, the literature of parental regret. Ruth's resentment of Angela and Rex is an "unmentionable thing," a secret "battened down so long that [it] had become almost unrecognizable as the truth." And yet Angela has always felt it; her life has been defined by "being rejected, abandoned, betrayed by someone who ought to love her." (Names shiver with symbolism throughout Mortimer's story: Ruth, in British English, means "repentance," "remorse," "regret." Rex is the cruel king of his sturdy, commuter-belt castle; during the week, he disappears Londonward to his job as a dentist, performing countless "careful excavations into rotting bone." Angela, meaning "messenger," is the character whose circumstances force Ruth into action.)

Mortimer doesn't theorize or expound; she lacerates, instead, with description. Her 65-year-old novel is, through its atmosphere and circumstance, one of the most compelling arguments for freedom of reproductive choice that I've ever encountered. Without choice, she suggests, we're condemned to follow tramlines of predestination that punish everyone involved. Without choice, everyone suffers, including the children born not out of love but resentment. (In the novel, Angela has always sensed how differently both her parents seem to regard her compared with her two younger brothers, both born by choice.) Ruth's psyche in the book is inexorably stunted by her inability to define herself before she had children. Reading Mortimer, I was reminded again and again of Merritt Tierce's 2021 *New York Times* essay—published decades after *Daddy's Gone a-Hunting* was written—outlining what getting pregnant at 19 had cost her. "My personhood was erased," she wrote, "and overwritten with MOTHER before I even knew who I was."

To deprive women of the ability to choose when and whether they become parents, the novel insinuates, is to deprive them of the ability to ever be or become fully human in their own right. In one chapter, Angela lies sleeping while Mortimer sketches out a surreal scene in which the teenager seems to have a conversation with her subconscious:

> What does myself look like? I mean, who am I?
>
> You are an examination result, dear. Perhaps, in time, an Honours Degree. Try harder.
>
> But myself—I mean myself?
>
> Perhaps you could find yourself in the Guides, or in the New Testament somewhere. If not, we can provide various substitutes, such as Joan of Arc, Florence Nightingale, Nurse Cavell. It's really none of our business, but we do keep a few heroines handy, just in case.

Angela's unformed sense of self is mirrored in the novel by Ruth's childlike state. "For the first time in their history, women are becoming aware of an identity crisis in their own lives," Friedan wrote in 1963, "a crisis which . . . will not end until they, or their daughters, turn an unknown corner and make of themselves and their own lives the new image that so many women now so desperately need." The moment, she argued, was "a turning point from an immaturity that has become femininity to full human identity." As harsh as Mortimer's exploration of motherhood might be, there are discernible signs of change on the horizon. Angela never for a moment considers marrying her awful boyfriend and keeping her baby, as her mother had done before her. When Ruth asks her if she wants to have an abortion, Angela is "bewildered, like someone asked whether they wanted to go on living." Ruth is easily able to tap into a whisper network of women offering advice and endorsements: "There was some Irishman, Susan Raynes said he was a real angel," one friend tells her. "Then Yvonne used to swear by some man in Chelsea somewhere." She has other recommendations too: Epsom salts; "something you can put on cotton wool"; soap.

With even the most longed-for baby, the identity shift into motherhood is necessarily painful, a sloughing-off of old needs, priorities, and desires accompanied by the primal absorption of another soul, another physical body into yourself. "Bone of your bones, curious flesh of your flesh," Ruth thinks. "Not a hair, not a fingernail, not a particle of skin is the same as it was at the moment of birth, but still the aging body that was once a child is part of you." The love Ruth has for Angela is elemental and difficult. Still, it drives her to help Angela make the choice that Ruth herself couldn't: the choice not to have the baby that would deny her a future of being anything but a mother.

A

WHAT THE SEXUAL VIOLENCE
OF *GAME OF THRONES* BEGOT

May 2021

I DON'T HAVE MUCH TOLERANCE these days for scenes involving the casual, ritualistic degradation of women, which is why deciding to rewatch *Game of Thrones* was such a colossal unforced error. *Idiotic! Foolhardy! Own goal!* I made it through the first episode, where a sobbing Daenerys Targaryen is raped by Khal Drogo on their wedding night in front of a romantic orange sunset. I got through the part where Daenerys learns to get her rapist to be nicer to her by being more of an engaged participant in her own sexual assault, and the moment where she subsequently falls in love with him and he with her. I watched as Ros is forced to violently beat another woman with a scepter to gratify the sadistic sexual predilections of King Joffrey, and as Brienne is dragged away to be gang-raped by Roose Bolton's soldiers, until Jaime saves her. I stopped watching shortly before Jaime rapes his sister, Cersei, next to their son's dead body, and before Sansa is raped by Ramsay Bolton while Theon Greyjoy watches. It occurred to me at some point that this was becoming an ordeal, and I could rewatch *New Girl* for a third time instead, where the only instance of sexualized violence is a comedic sub-plot involving Schmidt's accidentally broken penis.

Game of Thrones, which debuted 10 years ago this spring, has the dubious honor of being the ne plus ultra of rape culture on television. No series before, or since, has so flagrantly served up rape and assault simply for kicks, without a shadow of a nod toward "realism" (because *dragons*). The genre is fantasy, and the fantasy at hand is a world in which every woman, no matter her power or fortune, is likely to be violated in front of our eyes. Rape is like blood on *Game of Thrones*, so commonplace that viewers become inured to it, necessitating ever more excess to grab our attention. It's brutal, graphic, and hollow. It's also intentional. Daenerys's wedding night isn't explicitly written as being nonconsensual in George R. R. Martin's 1996 novel (despite the fact that the character was 13 at the time), and it wasn't filmed as such in the first, unreleased *Game of Thrones* pilot. At some point, the decision was made to introduce viewers to the series's most significant female character via her humiliating assault—with pornified aesthetics for added titillation—by a man who had purchased her.

When *Thrones* was on the air, each season brought with it ample discussion of its wearying reliance on rape for dramatic fodder. There have been exhaustive, character-by-character breakdowns of the exaggerated and invented instances of sexualized violence that the show's creators,

David Benioff and D. B. Weiss, introduced in adapting the show; in response to widespread criticism, Weiss and Benioff eventually toned down depictions of rape and assault and sacrificed neither viewership nor *Holy shit* watercooler moments in the process, proving the show never needed them in the first place.

A show treating sexual violence as casually now as *Thrones* did then is nearly unimaginable. And yet rape, on television, is as common as ever, sewn into crusading feminist tales and gritty crime series and quirky teenage dramedies and schlocky horror anthologies. It's the trope that won't quit, the Klaxon for supposed narrative fearlessness, the device that humanizes "difficult" women and adds supposed texture to vulnerable ones. Many creators who draw on sexual assault claim that they're doing so because it's so commonplace in culture and always has been. "An artist has an obligation to tell the truth," Martin once told *The New York Times* about why sexual violence is such a persistent theme in his work. "My novels are epic fantasy, but they are inspired by and grounded in history. Rape and sexual violence have been a part of every war ever fought." So have gangrene and post-traumatic stress disorder and male sexual assault, and yet none of those feature as pathologically in his "historical" narratives as the brutal rape of women.

Some progress is visible. Many writers, mostly men, continue to rely on rape as a nuclear option for female characters, a tool with which to impassion viewers, precipitate drama, and stir up controversy. Others, mostly women, treat sexual assault and the culture surrounding it as their subject, the nucleus around which characters revolve and from which plotlines extend. Rape as a trope, a joke—I could never encounter these devices again and sleep better for it. But in the hands of artists who want to deconstruct the idea of the rape plot altogether, we see a version of storytelling that serves us, and survivors, something more transformative.

STILL MORE COMMON, THOUGH, is the series that mistakes graphically portraying rape for having something insightful to say about it. At one point in the fourth season of *The Handmaid's Tale*, June (played by Elisabeth Moss) recounts in detail some of the assaults inflicted on her as a handmaid in Gilead, a merciless Christian theocracy in the show's alternate version of America. Her list is long, and yet not as long as the one I made while thinking about the show's historical treatment of assault. Over three previous seasons, viewers have watched June be raped by Commander Waterford (Joseph Fiennes); have nonconsensual sex with Nick (Max Minghella), followed by consensual sex when she later falls in love with him (there's that trope again); be raped by Waterford while nine months pregnant; be raped by Commander Lawrence (Bradley Whitford) when Waterford orders it; and murder Commander Winslow (Christopher Meloni) after he attempts to rape her. We've also seen female characters suffer genital mutilation, have their eyes taken out, be beaten with straps, and have fingers removed. The current season presents a 14-year-old who's already been raped by multiple men, the prolonged torture of June after she's recaptured (*yet again*) by Gilead, and a different hand-maid who develops romantic feelings for a man who's assaulted her.

I'll remind you that Hulu markets this show as a feminist fable. A trailer for the latest season that was released in 2020 features a character saying "Blessed be the squad," as if to borrow some of Alexandria Ocasio-Cortez's radical chic. The show's 2017 debut mere months into the Trump-Pence administration aligned it with ideas of a female-led resistance against patriarchal overreach. I loved the first season, the cool painterliness of the show's aesthetic and the thought experiment it offered about American puritanism, unleashed and institutionalized. But the longer the show went on—fueled, paradoxically, by the critical success of that first season—the more it became simply a series about the abuse of women. Nothing more, nothing less.

The second season made clear that its only objective was to keep people watching. The violence the show inflicts upon its characters delivers no overarching message, no moment of transcendence. In Gilead, sexual violence is a categorical imperative, and June and her allies are beaten and raped and tortured until they escape; when they're inevitably recaptured they are beaten and raped and tortured again. Unlike Margaret Atwood's 1985 novel, on which the series is based and in which June's "ceremony" with the Commander is described in clinical, disassociated language, the sexual violence of the show is cruel and up-close. Your tolerance for it depends on you. In one scene in the new season, June is waterboarded while Aunt Lydia uneasily does needlepoint in the hallway outside, and it occurred to me that viewers are essentially adopting Lydia's role, spectators tacitly encouraging the characters' prolonged abuse, uncomfortable but silent. Meanwhile the show's writers, not content with tormenting June, are increasingly portraying her as a problematic antihero, encouraging viewers to condemn her for being emotionally and psychologically undone for everything they've put her through.

In 2018, I wrote that *The Handmaid's Tale* had crossed the line into exploitation for its repeated victimization of its characters. In the fourth season, Moira (Samira Wiley) expresses a wish to "take all the shit from Gilead and turn it into something useful," an unintentionally apt summary of the show's primary failure. Usefulness is also lacking in the most vile scene in Amazon's recent horror series *Them*, a 1950s-set drama in which racism and supernatural forces terrorize a Black family. In the fifth episode, a flashback details the violent gang rape of the show's female protagonist, Lucky (Deborah Ayorinde), as her baby is murdered in front of her in a monstrous kind of game. The episode was written by two men: the show's creator, Little Marvin, and the playwright Dominic Orlando. It feels peculiarly grotesque to me that both so viscerally imagine and stage a scene that neither of them could ever experience—the twofold torture of a woman whose own rape becomes almost incidental to her compared with the loss of her child. It does nothing but appall, its evil too unsubtle to nurture anything but shock.

My colleague Hannah Giorgis, writing about *Them*, stated that "the sheer intensity and meaninglessness of the cruelty on display lends credence to arguments that Little Marvin didn't anticipate how the show might affect Black audiences, many of whom view it as a bloodied funhouse mirror of an already-horrifying reality." The argument that Marvin and *The Handmaid's Tale* showrunner, Bruce Miller, have made in defense of their work is that they're simply portraying what racist sexual violence and institutionalized sexual violence can and have looked like. But this thesis assumes we don't already know what this looks like, and ignores the fact that both men are simultaneously turning their subjects into entertainment, and profit. For all the criticism it garnered over the years, *Game of Thrones* was a ratings juggernaut, and many creators since have assumed that its willingness to dole out gratuitous sex and violence was the reason. But the era of peak TV has also mandated excess for new shows trying to break through: In a frantically crowded TV market-place, the more shocking you can be, the more people pay attention.

THE TIME HAS LONG since come, I think, to stop watching any show that treats sexual assault cheaply or as any kind of temporary narrative hot potato to be picked up and rapidly discarded. Rape shouldn't be a motivating force for a male character (*The Sopranos*, *True Detective*), a hum-bling or instigating force for an unlikable character (*House of Cards*, *Bates Motel*, *Private Practice*, *The Americans*), or a casual expression of tastelessness (pick any season of *American Horror Story*). Writers should stop imagining female characters falling in love with rapists, a trope that began with Laura and Luke on *General Hospital* and has persisted ever since, on *The Handmaid's Tale*, *The Fall*, and *Orange Is the New Black*, justifying assault as a twisted kind of courtship. Writers who don't identify as women or who have no first- or secondhand experience with sexual assault should consider carefully why they want to add it to a show, and should have to defend their impulses in doing so. The strange value of *Game of Thrones* is that it highlighted how tediously prestige television has come to rely on rape, both as titillation and as a catchall traumatic event that even the most lauded shows overuse to enable male heroism and character development.

That doesn't mean rape has to become a taboo subject. Critics have been divided over *Promising Young Woman*, which won an Oscar in 2021 for Best Original Screenplay, but the movie by Emerald Fennell breaks all kinds of traditions in using assault as a subject—it never shows violation on camera, it suggests that rapists are less-commonly evil serial abusers than banal office-types in button-downs, and it offers no redemptive arc for anyone. The movie begins and ends in a world mired in rape culture. HBO's *I May Destroy You*, which aired in 2020, was less a drama about rape than a way for an artist, Michaela Coel, to write her way through it; the show explored the limits of consent and the in-between instances of assault that aren't usually clarified by television. Watching HBO up to its premiere, you could have been forgiven for understanding rape as simply the violent sexual abuse of a woman. *I May Destroy You*, more gratifyingly, reframed it as a series of realistic violations—the stealthy removal of a condom during sex, a con played to trick a woman into a three-some, a consensual encounter between two men that becomes assault when the word *no* is ignored.

Above all, the question that writers should ask themselves, and that viewers should weigh, is why a rape is appearing onscreen or onstage in a work of art. When it is, it should be written, or at the very least talked through, with women or those with lived experience on the subject, who have enough power to challenge it. It should do more than simply exploit a real-life scourge for dramatic reasons. It should be able to make the staggering number of people who've survived sexual violence feel something more than pain when they watch.

RED CLOCKS IMAGINES
AMERICA WITHOUT ABORTION

February 2018

THE AMERICA IN LENI ZUMAS'S new novel, *Red Clocks*, is so familiar as to be almost unremarkable. Ro, a history teacher, has a father in a retirement home in Florida and a brother who died of a heroin overdose. Susan, a mother, raises two children in the house she grew up in. Gin, a loner, is defiantly private but offers home remedies to local women with health issues but no money or insurance. Mattie, a teenager, loses her virginity to a confident and callous classmate who's unconcerned with her comfort and doesn't wear protection. The only tweak Zumas has made is that in the world of her book abortion has been criminalized in the U.S., an occurrence introduced so quietly and so plausibly that it isn't even startling—just another calamity for women to add to the list.

Zumas switches fluently through the perspectives of each of these women in *Red Clocks*, which is set in the fictional small town of Newville, Oregon. Like an Elizabeth Strout novel, their personal stories and heartbreak layers into something more acute when women wake up one day to find that a president they didn't vote for—a man with a history of extreme rhetoric and legislation on reproductive issues—has proposed a Personhood Amendment to the U.S. Constitution, which a majority of states then vote to ratify.

Abortion, or the sudden illegality of it, is the novel's grounding hypothesis, but it isn't its primary focus. Zumas has written a work that's preoccupied with what it means to live inside a woman's body, and to exist in that body in a world that's long viewed it with fear and unease. And to handle a biological imperative that seems sometimes incompatible with other ambitions. And to experience the myriad small humiliations and the pain of the body's physical state. In the first scene, Ro is visiting a fertility specialist, described as "a room for women whose bodies are broken." At 42, Ro is many things: a teacher, a daughter, a writer working on the biography of a 19th-century Faroese polar explorer called Eivør Mínervudottír. In the doctor's office, though, she's defined only by her failure to fulfill her "animal destiny," and her "elderly pregravid" status as a patient. Ro tries repeatedly to understand why she wants so badly to be a mother, but it's an impulse she can't quantify, a desire she can't rationalize.

In the world of the novel, the same administration that's criminalized abortion has also outlawed IVF, since fertilized eggs can't give their consent to be moved from laboratory to uterus. It has also introduced new legislation called Every Child Needs Two, which requires that adoptive parents be married. As a single woman, Ro's last chance to have a child is artificial insemination, requiring drugs that leave her dizzy and exhausted, and that her insurance doesn't cover. On the flip side of her reality is Mattie, herself adopted, who's pregnant at 15 and out of options. Terminating a pregnancy is now classified as conspiracy to commit murder, and Mattie has already seen her best friend, the daughter of a state representative, jailed after she tried to self-abort rather than jeopardize her mother's career. In the abortion ban's early days, the book explains, women were prosecuted particularly harshly to help the legislation take effect, and "girls as young as 13 were incarcerated for three to five years."

The cleverness of Zumas's narrative structure is that it allows readers to understand the characters both from their own perspective and as they exist in the minds of others. Their names are introduced late into their stories; until then, Zumas refers to them as "The Biographer" (Ro), "The Daughter" (Mattie), "The Mender" (Gin), and "The Wife" (Susan), in a nod to the singular categories women can be shoehorned into. Gin is revealed as a woman who loves to fix people and animals, a person with kind instincts who feels things deeply, not least of which is the impulse to isolate herself. It's only when she's seen by other characters that she becomes an outcast, a hermit whom the local fishermen suspect of witchcraft. Similarly, Susan and Ro judge each other's lifestyles and choices, making presumptions that are soon challenged by the other's narration.

What this all builds into is a thoughtful, complicated picture of womanhood—and a fierce argument for individual choice. The reality Zumas conceives is much like the reality of any society where abortion is outlawed: Deprived of options, women go to increasingly desperate and unsafe lengths to end their pregnancies. Teenagers fleeing to Canada face the "Pink Wall," a diplomatic agreement that allows border police to detain and forcibly test any woman or girl whom they suspect to be seeking an abortion. Without access to comprehensive sexual education, Mattie and her friends share old wives' tales and snippets of hearsay that invariably fail them. But something else happens, too. Women like Gin become de facto healthcare providers, offering remedies that Ro describes as being "thousands of years in the making, fine-tuned by women in the dark creases of history, helping each other." Activist groups emerge with names like the "Polyphonte Collective," which nod to the forbidding history of women being punished for their reproductive decisions.

That *Red Clocks* does all this while portraying the everyday existence of four such different characters in persuasive, gripping language is striking. Zumas isn't an idealist—she's fully aware of the ways in which women think about each other, and the conditioning that turns minor encounters into contests or conflicts. But she's also steeped her book in history, which fills in the gaps between her characters. Gin is descended from Maria Hallett, an 18th-century woman abandoned by a pirate whose reclusiveness led to her being labeled as a witch. Ro is obsessed with uncovering the life story of Mínervudottír, whose biographical fragments precede each chapter, and who couldn't stop striving for an extraordinary life, a life "in which survival was not assured."

Zumas, an author and professor of creative writing at Portland State University, reportedly based some of the novel on her own experiences undergoing fertility treatment. In these chapters, *Red Clocks* is relentlessly interrogative but always humane. Ro asks herself over and over again why she wants to be a mother, and can only answer, *Because I do.* The desire, she deduces, must come from "some creaturely place, pre-civilized, some biological throb that floods her bloodways with the message *Make more of yourself.*" But even in her most desperate moments Ro never lets her desires supersede anyone else's. The paradox of fertility, where teenagers procreate effortlessly against their wills and adult women with means find they've left it too late, is a bittersweet joke in Ro's mind, but not one she's willing to compromise other women's choices for—her own difficulty conceiving doesn't change her belief that every women should have autonomy over her own body.

With such a provocative premise, you might expect this to be an activist novel, or a polemical one. But the political circumstances of the novel are sidelined to only the most essential moments of exposition, in snatches of memories about women's marches (and a fleeting mention that PBS has lost its government funding and is forced to air commercials for control-top panty hose). *Red Clocks* instead is deeply, intentionally personal. Rather than trafficking in sweeping generalizations or one-size-fits-all dictates, it focuses on the uniqueness of all of its characters, who are nevertheless linked by the immutability of their bodies. The familiarity of the book's world, just a step removed from our own reality, is the most shocking thing about it.

A

THE DARK SIDE
OF FITNESS CULTURE

June 2021

THIS IS SUPPOSED TO BE the season of unleashed, exuberant exhibitionism. Many of us have swaddled our pale bodies in Lycra and terry cloth for more than a year; the theory of Hot Vax Summer is that we're long overdue to expose them to the cruel light of other people's eyes. In the music video for "Solar Power," Lorde basks on the beach in a lemon-yellow crop top, the symmetry of her rib cage its own work of art. "Forget all of the tears that you've cried; it's over," she sings, shooing away our literal and metaphorical winter of COVID-19. (Predictably, the outfit she wears—$615 plus tax!—sold out immediately.) I watched most of *Physical*—Apple TV+'s new series about a 1980s aerobics queen-in-waiting—with this in mind, idly running my hand over and over my unsculpted midriff, fighting the impulse to throw on a leotard and sweat joyfully along to "Space Age Love Song." This is the conflict at the center of American consumerist fitness spectacle: Even when it's at its most transparently questionable, the promise is almost impossible to resist.

Physical, created by the playwright Annie Weisman, digs into a window of history, when making people hate their body became a thriving pillar of American commerce. It's a strikingly beautiful show about ugly things: self-hatred, mental illness, rampant capitalism, politics, the Summer of Love gone to seed. The directors, who include Craig Gillespie (*I, Tonya*; *Cruella*), render the San Diego setting with sun-dappled luminosity; the overall aesthetic is somewhere between beachy '70s hedonism and brittle '80s plasticity. Sheila (played by Rose Byrne) is a housewife with an eating disorder so virulent, it gets its own accompanying monologue, also delivered by Byrne. While Sheila stares at her reflection in the opening scene, her permed curls popping against green patterned wallpaper, the voice calls her pathetic for trying to carry off "the disco-sex-kitten look at your age." When she runs errands, it reminds her that she's "pale, pasty, fat, gross, disgusting." During a discussion about an upcoming dinner party with her uninterested husband, it tells her, "You're the only one who thinks about food this much, you fucking freak."

The writer and body-acceptance activist Katie Sturino calls this kind of inner voice "a self-shit-talking spiral." It's almost as unpleasant for viewers to endure as it must be for Sheila; critics have lamented the show's pitch-black tone and Sheila's judgmental gaze, which is sharpest when she directs it toward herself. Maybe the popular assumption was that a Reagan-era dramedy about the VHS home-fitness boom would be as tonally giddy as Netflix's *GLOW*, or as deliberately nostalgic as *Stranger Things*. Defined by Weisman, who based Sheila's interior life partly on her own experiences with an eating disorder, *Physical* is something else instead. Dark and caustic, it's also unnervingly clear-sighted about the ways people really see themselves, and the money they'll spend for just the promise of deliverance. After watching Sheila teach her first aerobics class and shout tough-love slogans at her students, her fellow instructor Bunny (Della Saba) looks reluctantly impressed. "People usually want to be cuddled in this country," she says. But Sheila, the show promises in a flash-forward to a glitzy VHS shoot, is about to make a fortune by projecting her own insecurities and self-loathing out into the homes of millions.

BYRNE PLAYS SHEILA A bit like a rubber band stretched to its fracturing point, so tense she almost vibrates. Her husband, Danny (Rory Scovel), is a wormy academic who plays on Sheila's lack of confidence to get her to arrange a threesome with one of his students; he's so lazy that he even outsources the seduction to his wife. Sheila spends virtually the entirety of her waking life thinking about wanting to eat. Her 4-year-old daughter is an afterthought; she has no friends. Her only hobbies are going to a ballet studio that closes in the first episode, and renting a motel room where she methodically eats her way through three cheeseburgers, vomits, showers, and then sits meditatively between sheets that still smell of grease.

But when Sheila first discovers aerobics, via a seemingly carefree blond woman whom she stalks from a mall parking lot into a class, something changes. The music, the beat, the quick-changing sequences—they occupy her mind, allowing her to move and forget herself until the class ends. *Physical* captures the frenetic release that she feels in a montage of cuts back and forth. At home, her fingers drum frantically on the kitchen counter; in the studio, her hips circle around and around in sensuous, undulating bliss.

Sheila seems obviously inspired by Jane Fonda. Both come from wealthy and difficult families (one episode reveals a traumatic incident from Sheila's past that offers an explanation for why she's so unhappy); Fonda also lived with bulimia, from her teens until her 40s. Like Sheila, Fonda attended ballet class to keep fit, until she injured her foot on a film set and, in 1978, began practicing aerobics. The workouts, she told *Slate*'s Willa Paskin in a riveting episode of the podcast *Decoder Ring*, filled the hole that her eating disorder occupied in her life. In 1982, she released *Jane Fonda's Workout*, a groundbreaking video aimed at bringing aerobics to women who couldn't or didn't want to go to a studio. It sold more than 17 million copies and spawned a home-fitness empire, not to mention a sticky fitness motto, shouted gleefully by Fonda, mid-lunge: "No pain, no gain."

Sheila taps into this sentiment, and the show promises that it's what will make her an icon. (Somewhat irritatingly, the entire season suffers from the Peak TV complaint of prologue-itis, with the real juicy stuff likely saved for Season 2.) The more Sheila channels her destructive inner monologue into her classes, exhorting her students to embrace discomfort, the "sweet spot" where real change happens, the fewer her cruel voice-overs become. It's cathartic for her, as it clearly was for Fonda. But what about the rest of us? What happens when you grow up internalizing the idea that judging yourself is normal and quieted only with excessive effort? What becomes of an entire culture raised on the argument that our troublesome, too-big, too-weak, too-much bodies can be loved only when they've been conquered?

THE ONLY CERTAIN ASPECT of the first pandemic year is that everyone's experience has been different. COVID-19 sharpened inequities in capital, but also safety. It clarified how fragile social-support networks can be, how disproportionately mothers bear the brunt of schools and child care shutting down, how the ability to take optimal care of our bodies is a privilege not everyone has. And yet somehow one of the dominant messages of the current moment, as many Americans are reentering the world, isn't that society needs to change, but that our bodies do. The pandemic, one *New York Times* article from March scolded, is "a wake-up call for personal health." Quarantine weight gain, according to WebMD, is "not a joking matter." Gwyneth Paltrow popped up in March 2021 confessing that she'd gained 14 pounds in quarantine by indulging in bread and alcohol—not to be relatable, but to help hawk a diet book dedicated to "intuitive fasting."

Here is my story: I gained 37 pounds during the pandemic because I was pregnant, and lost 30 of them the first month after having twins because I was so exhausted and anxious and depressed that I didn't eat. The other seven pounds stayed with me. In January, I tried "intermittent fasting," which is basically the same thing as starving, only with a timetable. It worked, in the sense that I lost a few more pounds, but it also became my obsession. I thought about nothing but eating. I inhaled recipe books and food blogs on weekends like a day trader doing lines in a Pearl Street–bar toilet. Eventually there came a point when I didn't want to waste so much of my mental energy thinking about food, or craving food. My body is fine. It's strong. I can hold two 20-pound babies at the same time. I'll never wear an "extreme crop top" (thank you again, *New York Times*!) but I can eat three meals a day and free my mind for something, anything, else.

Watching *Physical*, with its access into the exhausting obsessiveness of Sheila's mind, I kept thinking about the argument that the since-gone-depressingly-conspiratorial Naomi Wolf made in *The Beauty Myth* that self-loathing is what society uses to keep women from organizing for what they actually desire:

> It's true what they say about women: Women *are* insatiable. We *are* greedy. Our appetites do need to be controlled if things are to stay in place. If the world were ours too, if we believed we could get away with it, we *would* ask for more love, more sex, more money, more commitment to children, more food, more care. These sexual, emotional, and physical demands *would* begin to extend to social demands: payment for care of the elderly, parental leave, childcare, etc. The force of female desire would be so great that society would truly have to reckon with what women want.

Physical tells just one part of this story, from one moment in time. It presents us with a character who finds in exercise a release from her own darkest impulses. But it also exposes how commonplace those impulses are, and how easy it is to capitalize on them. Hot Vax Summer should feel like liberation, not a prescription for what supposedly ails us. I came away from *Physical* with a question—what if we didn't want to look the way we've always been told we should look by a $78 billion industry with a very vested interest in supplying an unattainable ideal: sinewy and razor-hipped, hairless and waist-trained and uncomfortable? What are all the other things we could want instead? Where would we even begin?

ARTICLE CREDITS

"The Literary-Abuser Trope Is Everywhere" copyright © 2021 by The Atlantic Monthly Group LLC

"The Problem With Emily Ratajkowski's *My Body*" copyright © 2021 by The Atlantic Monthly Group LLC

"Curse of the '90s Bombshell" copyright © 2022 by The Atlantic Monthly Group LLC

"The Unending Assaults on Girlhood" copyright © 2021 by The Atlantic Monthly Group LLC

"The Ballad of Taystee Jefferson" copyright © 2019 by The Atlantic Monthly Group LLC

"Making Peace with Jane Austen's Marriage Plots" copyright © 2017 by The Atlantic Monthly Group LLC

"The Soft Radicalism of Erotic Fiction" copyright © 2021 by The Atlantic Monthly Group LLC

"The Remarkable Rise of the Feminist Dystopia" copyright © 2018 by The Atlantic Monthly Group LLC

"The Calamity of Unwanted Motherhood" copyright © 2022 by The Atlantic Monthly Group LLC

"What The Sexual Violence of *Game of Thrones* Begot" copyright © 2021 by The Atlantic Monthly Group LLC

"*Red Clocks* Imagines America Without Abortion" copyright © 2018 by The Atlantic Monthly Group LLC

"The Dark Side of Fitness Culture" copyright © 2021 by The Atlantic Monthly Group LLC

A

ABOUT THE AUTHOR

SOPHIE GILBERT is a staff writer at *The Atlantic* where she writes about television, books, and popular culture. She was a finalist for the 2022 Pulitzer Prize in Criticism. Before joining *The Atlantic* in 2014, she was the arts editor at *Washingtonian*, where she won three Society of Professional Journalists awards for arts reporting and criticism. She has previously written for *The New York Times*, *The Washington Post*, *The New Republic*, and *The Brooklyn Rail*.